To Susan
From Cici E
X Mas 1997

AMERICAN COUNTRY LIVING

CHRISTMAS

RECIPES, CRAFTS, AND MORE

AMERICAN COUNTRY LIVING

CHRISTMAS

RECIPES, CRAFTS, AND MORE

BARBARA RANDOLPH

ARCH CAPE PRESS

New York

A FRIEDMAN GROUP BOOK

Copyright © 1991 by Michael Friedman Publishing Group, Inc.

This 1991 edition published by Arch Cape Press,
distributed by Outlet Book Company, Inc.,
a Random House Company,
225 Park Avenue South,
New York, New York 10003.

ISBN 0-517-02014-9

AMERICAN COUNTRY LIVING: CHRISTMAS
was prepared and produced by
Michael Friedman Publishing Group, Inc.
15 West 26th Street
New York, New York 10010

Editor: Sharon Kalman
Art Director: Jeff Batzli
Layout and Illustrations: Helayne Messing
Photography Researcher: Daniella Jo Nilva

Typeset by Bookworks Plus
Color separation by Scantrans Pte. Ltd.
Printed and bound in Hong Kong by Leefung-Asco Printers, Ltd.

8 7 6 5 4 3 2 1

Additional photo credits:

© Hanson Carroll: 12–13, 102–103
© Hanson Carroll/FPG International: 78–79
© Martha McBride/Unicorn Stock Photos: 22–23
© Obrien & Mayor/FPG International: 94–95
© Ralph B. Pleasant/FPG International: 112–113
© Anita Sabarese: 62–63

DEDICATION

To my neighbor, Dixie, in whose home the spirit of Christmas is alive all through the year.

© Hanson Carroll

CONTENTS

THE ESSENCE OF A COUNTRY CHRISTMAS

A country Christmas delights all the senses. Its essence hangs in the air with the pungency of balsam, the smell of pies in the oven, the hint of wood smoke, and the scent of drying mittens. It is the bubbling sound of laughter, caroling, sleigh bells, church bells, and the stamping of snow from boots. It is the taste of rich spices, cranberries, and peppermint sticks. It is the cold of a snowflake on your nose, the warmth of a mug of mulled cider. Its look is simple, homespun, and natural. It is deep greens accented in red, bright primaries tempered in warm earth tones.

A country Christmas is a state of mind not attached to any place. Just as the countryside itself varies in climate, landscape, and style, so does its Christmas. Luminarias, traditional Mexican Christmas lanterns made from a brown paper bag with a lighted candle inside, now lead the way up snow-filled New England driveways, just as fir trees from the Maine woods glow with lights and tinsel in parlors of the Deep South. In the same sense, the doorway of a big-city apartment can welcome guests into an atmosphere of pure country Christmas inside.

A country Christmas stirs the remembrance of Christmases past, and on it are built the memories that will endure a lifetime. It gives repose to the soul that only home and memories of it can bring. For home is what a country

Christmas is all about: living in it, decorating it, filling it with the smells of good things in the oven, taking comfort and joy in it, and welcoming guests into it.

A country Christmas evokes a strong feeling of nature brought indoors. There are no all-blue-decorated trees, no trendy cuteness of "theme rooms." Christmas here comes straight from the heart, an eclectic celebration drawn from traditions well worn and long cherished.

Simple, natural lines and traditional decorating styles, rich in the folk arts of each family's ethnic heritage, are hallmarks of the country Christmas. The bounty of the woods and fields, home-cooked goodness, and homespun gifts from the heart are the ingredients.

Few things in life are as dear as the traditions of Christmas and no matter where or how you celebrate it, you can create your own traditions that will last a lifetime.

The hearth and mantel are a focal point for the entire room.

© Hanson Carroll

Ribbon bows bring the gift theme to the tree itself.

CHAPTER ONE

PREPARING FOR CHRISTMAS

The easy atmosphere and relaxed pace tinged with anticipation that characterize Christmas in the country are not accidental. The country year is, perforce, one of seasons and to each belongs its own activities. If the time before Christmas seems more relaxed than others, it is possibly because it follows one of the year's busiest seasons.

The harvest that begins with the first pink chive blossom in the spring lasts until the snow lies deep upon the garden. And as the fruits and flowers of summer are all carefully preserved, so begins the preparation for Christmas. The most sparkling jar of pickles is set aside for Christmas dinner, glowing jellies and herb-rich vinegars are put away to fill gift baskets, and the everlasting flowers that will grace wreaths have been a part of that harvest all through summer and fall. By December they are collected and ready. Now all that needs to be done is to prepare the fruits of your labor—making the wreaths, pickling the cucumbers—most of which can be done at your leisure throughout the summer and fall months.

© Hanson Carroll

PLANNING AHEAD

In the well-ordered country home there will always be at least a few homemade gifts ready and tucked away in the closet under the eaves—wool mittens knit in February and March, sachets made from the needles saved from last year's tree, jars of potpourri made from June's roses, packets of the summer's herbs picked at their prime.

More than conscious planning, this is perhaps just the normal response to the offerings and opportunities of each season. The feel of wool slipping between knitting needles was comforting in February, the roses and chives were in bloom in June, and the cucumbers were just the right size for pickling in July. And so the well-stocked pantry and eaves closet was filled.

But even with these preliminaries accomplished, there are many things that must be done in those busy weeks before December twenty-fifth. The trick is to do these without feeling pressured or as though you are running at full speed only to always remain a few paces behind. Some serious planning is a must.

It helps to begin with a few lists of those things you feel must be done: gifts to assemble, decorations to make and display, cards to send, cookies to bake, packages to mail and deliver. Sort these into several lists in order of priority. Put those things you simply must do on the "priority one" list, the next most important on the "priority two" list. List these on separate pages of a small notebook. The rest of the notebook is a good place for noting what you plan to give to whom and other essentials it will be handy to have in one place.

If you sort these activities by priority, you are less likely to find yourself doing less important things first and rushing around at the last minute to do the essentials. Add a page of rewards—those things you love to do before the holidays, but seldom have a chance to do, like taking the children to see the animated windows, having a few friends in for an impromptu Sunday brunch, making everyone's favorite (but time-consuming) dinner or dessert. Resolve to do one of these whenever you cross a certain number of tasks off your list.

© Obrien & Mayor/FPG International

Brightly colored candies are an easy way to add a holiday accent to the home.

© Hanson Carroll

Keep it easy, fun, and manageable. Working the extra chores of the holidays into an already full schedule is never easy, so don't expect to do it all yourself. Christmas is not a one-man (or woman) show with you doing it all, nor is it a monthlong party thrown for the rest of the family by mother. Let everyone take part. Look carefully at your lists and share those chores that suit the schedules and talents of others.

Let a child wrap the gifts. So what if they are not exactly the way you would have done them—grandmother will be delighted at the original wrappings and the proud grand-child who created them. Give errands to others, have an older child address the envelopes for cards, leaving them for you to sign and add personal notes. Or don't send cards at all this year and write short notes after Christmas to far-away friends. Set your own priorities.

Make things more convenient by keeping materials handy. Put wrapping paper, ribbon, tags, scissors, and tape in a large basket next to the fireplace or under an end table. As gifts are finished or purchased, wrap them or give them to someone else to wrap, without having to haul out all the materials each time.

If you have children to wait for after school, or carpools to drive, carry your Christmas cards, a pen, your address book, and stamps with you in a little basket.

Along with lists of things to do, make lists of things to buy—gifts, wrappings, materials, ingredients—well in advance and pick them up as you see them instead of spending an exhausting day shopping or making separate last-minute trips. Begin stocking your pantry in the fall with those things you'll need extras of—nuts, chocolate chips, dried and candied fruits, sugar, and flour.

KEEP IT SIMPLE

Few things are fun if done in a hurry or under pressure. By simplifying your plans, you can leave yourself and your family time to enjoy Christmas. Keep your house uncluttered, too—it will save you time and give you a sense of space and calm instead of frenzy. Clear away other decorative items as you unpack and set up the crèche sets and other Christmas decorations, storing the year-round knickknacks in the boxes that held the holiday treasures. After Christmas, swap back. Instead of crowding the furniture together to make room for the Christmas tree, try removing a chair and storing it on an enclosed porch that isn't used in the winter or placing it in a bedroom or guest room.

Cook twice as much stew as you need for supper and put it away in the refrigerator to have two or three nights later. There is no law that says you can't have the same dish two nights in the same week. That leaves your kitchen and your time free for an evening's baking or relaxing by the fire to read a favorite story together. Plan more simple one-pot menus for the weeks before Christmas.

Think ahead to some of the dishes you will need for holiday meals and cook them ahead. Cranberry sauce keeps in the refrigerator for weeks and cornbread for stuffing can be frozen. Pâtés and cheese spreads for entertaining can be made a week in advance.

Group your activities together to avoid repeatedly getting out and putting away your half-finished projects. If you have a guest room or other place you can spare for a few weeks, use it as a Christmas studio and keep all your materials there. That will save cleanup time and allow you to leave works-in-progress where you can resume them.

This wide variety of sugar cookies came from one basic recipe.

© Floyd Jillson/FPG International

If you must work on the kitchen or dining room table, collect all the supplies for one type of project in a basket to make cleanup and preparation faster and easier. If you are making several stenciled gifts, for example, keep paints, brushes, stencils, tape, paper towels, and other supplies together. Or, if you are making homemade cards, keep scissors, paper, and other accessories together.

Don't plan to make *all* your gifts (unless you begin very early). Choose a few projects and finish one before starting the next. Otherwise, you may end up with all half-finished projects. Group similar activities together—cutting fabric and machine stitching, for instance—but be sure you are not beginning more projects than you can possibly finish.

By trying only a limited number of new crafts or techniques in one season, you will avoid getting your plans so complicated that you can't complete them all. If a project turns out to be more difficult and time-consuming than you had expected, put it away until after Christmas when you will have more time and energy. You'll have a good start on next year. Gift-giving, like parties, should be fun for the giver, too.

Simplify your Christmas entertaining as well. Plan informal get-togethers instead of full-course, sit-down dinners. Buffets are easier to plan, as are brunches. Invite everyone for "Just Desserts" in the evening or have a late party after a school concert or other evening event.

Plan cooperative social events: an old-fashioned potluck supper or a cookie swap where everyone brings a few dozen of their favorite cookies and goes home with a grand assortment. Or clear the decks and invite friends to join you in decorating sugar cookies you've baked ahead.

CHAPTER TWO

ALL THROUGH THE HOUSE

Each season has its own decorations—a swag of bright dried corn on the front door, a jack-o'-lantern grinning from the window, a bouquet of spring flowers on the table—but only Christmas fills the house with them.

Decorating the house for Christmas is a labor of love. It isn't a project you set about purposefully one day and complete on the spot.

Fresh greens appear an armful at a time and gradually fill the house with the scent. Baskets of ribbon and wrapping and greeting cards creep in, a big bowl of bright potpourri appears, and a row of pomanders is drying above the wood stove. Decorating for Christmas is more fun this way, instead of being an obstacle to overcome.

Throughout this chapter are suggestions and ideas for filling your home with Christmas. There are special sections on quick tricks you can do with greens, special ways to scent your home during this season, and decorating with candlelight. Use these ideas as a starting point and let your imagination run wild.

Even after the snow falls, you can gather some wild materials for decorating.

© Anita Sabarese

GATHERING WILD MATERIALS

Long before the snow falls, it is time to gather the cones, pods, dried grasses, and seeds that will become wreaths and ornaments. An early snow may cover these, making collection difficult or impossible, so it is best to do this early in the season.

While not everyone has their own "back forty" from which to gather materials, there are many alternatives. Since you won't be cutting wild greens or plants, nearly any open piece of land, except public lands established as nature reserves, will do. Friends' gardens, fields, wood lots, vacant lots, backyards, and roadsides will provide ample seeds, cones, and grasses. On a Sunday drive in the

country, armed with scissors and paper bags, you can collect plenty of material for your decorating projects.

Always cut or break off dried plants such as grasses and seed pods on stems. Never pull on the plant hoping that it will break off, since many of these have shallow roots and you could easily uproot the plant.

Look along roadsides and streets for cones and seeds from trees: the winged seeds of maple, beechnuts, buckeyes, acorns, and sweet gum pods are all beautiful on cone wreaths. Collect different varieties of cones. Even the large, ungainly ones can be used as bases or broken into lovely rosettes. Tiny cones such as hemlock and balsam make good fillers in potpourri as well as being the right size for miniature wreaths. Keep your eyes open; no matter where you live, you will find good material.

GATHERING GREENS

To gather greens in the woods (with the landowner's blessing, of course), use a pair of stout clippers or pruning shears and cut each branch at an angle. Never strip the branches from the tree. You will soon notice, if you are gathering balsam, that the branches at the top have fuller, more three-dimensional needle growth than those at the bottom, which are fairly flat. Both are good for wreaths and other uses, but the top greens make a fuller wreath with more depth.

Collect the boughs into bundles and tie them near the stem end for easier carrying. Remember that whatever jacket and gloves you wear are very likely to get pitch on them. A layer of newspapers will protect car seats from both pitch and falling needles. If you do not plan to use the boughs immediately, store them in a cool place, standing them up in a large bucket of water. Be sure to get them into the water as quickly as possible, before the cut ends seal over and prevent water intake. If this happens, cut the stems again, and put them in water immediately. If the greens are kept standing instead of being stacked they will maintain a more natural shape. Standing them also avoids crushing and breaking the needles.

Unused boughs should be discarded outdoors when they are no longer needed. They can become a serious fire hazard, particularly in a garage, if left to dry out. The same is true of wreaths after they are taken down.

EVERGREENS AND WREATHS

Evergreen boughs, either formed into wreaths or tied in swags, bundles, bouquets, or ropes, are the favorite Christmas decoration. For many, even those who live where evergreen is not plentiful, it simply is not Christmas without an evergreen wreath on the door.

Balsam is the favorite green to use during Christmas. Its pungent fragrance grows more intense as the season progresses, and its rich green color, short needles, and out-

Fir, pine, juniper, cedar, and holly combine to form this festive swag.

standing keeping qualities have earned it first place. In addition, it is often available already cut from Christmas tree sellers, who trim branches from trees or have damaged trees that they must discard. Balsam is also the best material for evergreen roping, since it holds its needles well even when cut into short sprigs.

Other greens work almost as well for wreathmaking and other decorations, and each has its own special qualities.

© Anita Sabarese

White pine, with its long, soft needles, makes a nice, full wreath, especially if you use a larger wreath frame as a base. On very small frames, its long needles tend to fill in the center. White pine is the preferred branch for door swags and baskets or vases of standing boughs. It is full, pliable, and mixes well with other greens as well as with berries such as bittersweet and alder.

Cedar has interesting foliage, unlike the needles of the pines and firs, and is a good green on its own or mixed with others, where its texture is a fine contrast. Its foliage is flat, making it a good base for combinations of fresh and dried materials.

Spruce and **hemlock** both have short needles that make handsome wreaths, but tend to begin losing their needles very quickly. They can be used in vases or arrangements where their stems can be kept in water. It is possible to make wreaths on a base that holds moisture, and this is the only method suitable for these two. **Blue spruce** is especially attractive, and contrasts well with the deeper greens of others.

Scotch pine would make a good wreath, but it is so stiff that it is nearly impossible to work with. In a swag it lacks the graceful flexibility of white pine or cedar.

Juniper can be used alone, but its needles are so short that it is best used in combination with other greens. Its pale color and white berries contrast well to darker greens, and its narrow, stiff shape works well in standing arrangements.

Monterey pine has shiny, bright green needles nearly twice the length of white pine needles, and a bit stiffer. A wreath of these would have to be quite large, but the branches are fine for standing arrangements.

QUICK TRICKS WITH GREENS

An armful of fresh-cut greens can transform your home in minutes.

Stand them in a basket in the front hall for a dramatic and fragrant greeting.

Tie several long branches together with a red bow and lay them across a table or buffet.

Make a bouquet of shorter branches and stand them in a vase.

Surround a bowl of fruit or other centerpiece with greens, tucking the cut ends out of sight.

Casually lay medium-sized branches across your windowsills, with or without bows.

Tie a bunch of greens together with red ribbon and hang it on the door or attach it horizontally over a doorway.

Tuck sprigs of greenery into bowls of fruit or decorate a dish of cookies with them.

Hang bundles of greens from the kitchen rafters as you would dried flowers.

And, until you have a minute to do all of these things, pile the cut greens into a wood-carrier and let them decorate while they wait!

A BASIC EVERGREEN WREATH

A crinkle-wire single-wreath frame

A spool of green florist's wire

Plenty of evergreen boughs

Clippers or strong scissors

Clip the tips of the boughs into sprigs, each about the same length. The larger your wreath, the longer these can be, but they should be uniform. Six to eight inches is a good length if you are making a small wreath. Be sure that there are no cut ends showing —all the tips should be natural ends. Assemble a large pile of these sprigs before you begin tying them into bundles. Although many wreathmakers simply tie the sprigs to the wire frame without tying each bundle first, beginners will find it less time-consuming in the long run to add this step. Wrap the wire two or three times around the stems of each group of three or four sprigs, and collect up a pile of these before beginning the wreath itself.

Lay the first bunch of greens alongside the top of the frame, stems pointing to the right (reverse this if you are left-handed). The stems should be parallel to the wire of the frame, not perpendicular to it. Tie the end of the wire securely to the frame and begin wrapping it around the frame and the stems of the greens, using two or three wraps of wire. Add a second bunch, this time inside the frame, but with the stems still facing to the left. Again, secure with a few wraps of wire.

Continue to add bunches of greens, each one covering the wrapping on the one before it, working around the frame and alternating between the inside and the outside of the frame. You may also need to place some bundles directly in the center to keep the wreath full. When you come full circle to the place where you began, you will have to pull back the ends of those first greens and work underneath them. Finish with several tight wraps of wire and leave a long tail for a hanging loop if desired.

Stand back from your wreath and look at it from a distance to be sure it is even. If there are bare places, or those where the greens are a little thinner or the wreath a little narrower, you can usually simply tuck a bundle or two of greens into the wreath, under the wire that is already there or between other stems.

The shape of your wreath will be determined by the length of the tips you cut. Longer ones will make larger, more open wreaths, while short ones will make narrower, more compact wreaths.

If you choose to mix the greens in your wreath, it is best to mix each little bunch. To make a double-faced wreath, one with greens on both sides, flip the wreath over after each bundle is added and wire one to the other side. Double wreaths are full and luxurious, but are sometimes too thick for the

© Hanson Carroll

space between the door and storm door.

When you have made a number of wreaths, you may wish to skip the step of tying the little bundles first, simply adding the bunches of sprigs and tying them on with the wire. Use whatever method gives you the best finished wreath.

You will most likely get pitch on your hands, so to clean your hands after working with evergreens, use lard or vegetable shortening. These are much easier on your hands than turpentine or most hand cleaners and you will not have to scrub—just rub it on and wipe it off. Then wash your hands with regular hand soap.

EVERGREEN SWAGS

The soft, pliable nature of white pine makes it perfect for the base of door swags, but any evergreen that lies fairly flat will do.

Medium-gauge florist's wire

Evergreen boughs 10 to 18 inches long, preferably a mix of several, such as white pine, cedar, balsam, juniper, and boxwood

Pinecones, one very large or three medium-size

Red all-weather ribbon

Lay three long sprays of white pine or other flat evergreen on a work surface. Lay three more medium-length boughs over them. Wrap their stems together with wire, spreading the greens gracefully.

Arrange shorter boughs (about half the length of the first group) of the same varieties of evergreen so they form a spray facing the other direction. Push the two groups together so the cut ends of each one are partly buried in the other. Wire the second group of stems to the first with several wraps.

Wire the pinecones together into a group (or use a single large cone) and place them over the long boughs, near the place where the stems meet. Wire the cones in place and fill in around them with shorter sprigs of evergreen to cover the stem section. Tie the ribbon into a bow—a multi-looped wire bow is usually best for these (see page 36 for information on how to make these)—leaving long streamers. Wire the bow to the swag, just above the pinecones, so it covers the wire. If necessary, add a few short sprigs to balance the design or cover any bare places. Trim the ribbon ends diagonally or with a notch, making them a little shorter than the long pine boughs.

Hang the swag on the door at a slight angle, with the longest boughs facing down. If the swag is in the sun, some of the needles may fall. If there are bare branches, simply pull these out carefully (put the swag on a flat surface first) and replace them with fresh ones pushed into the arrangement.

ROPES OF EVERGREEN

Long strings of evergreens are lovely and graceful when draped around mirrors, mantels, doors, and windows or spiraled around a banister or newel post. Although time-consuming, these ropes are not difficult to make. Cedar and white pine are the easiest greens to work with because they are flexible and long-lasting, but balsam makes a more fragrant rope and lasts quite well.

Soft cotton clothesline cord (stiff cords do not drape well)

Fine-gauge florist's wire

Short sprigs of evergreen

Measure the length of roping needed and mark it on the cord, but do not cut. Leave 2 feet of cord for tying before starting to measure. Tie one end of the cord to a fixed object: a table leg if you are working on the floor, or a doorknob.

Cut greens into 5 to 6 inch lengths and wrap three or four together into little bundles, their stems tied with wire. After a while you may decide to wire individual sprigs directly to the cord, but at first this extra step makes the job a lot easier.

Wire the bundles to the cord so that each bunch covers the stems of the previous one. Work around the cord in a spiral so the evergreen covers the cord evenly. Make a half knot in the wire after every

few bunches to keep them from coming unwrapped when you set it down. You can make the rope thicker or thinner by increasing and decreasing the bundles used per foot of cord.

After you have finished the length needed, go back to the beginning and cover the stems of the first few with very short sprigs wired in the opposite direction. Push their stems into the main part of the roping and hide the wire under the needles.

These ropes can be highlighted by spiraled strings of cranberries or unbuttered and unsalted popcorn. Cranberries should only be used close to the holidays or they will need to be replaced, since they become soft quickly. Do not string cranberries and popcorn together, since the cranberry juice will run all over the popcorn and ruin it. Use a strong thread and a heavy needle to string either of these. Run the needle through the popcorn slightly to one side in order to avoid any hard kernels in the center.

© Steven Mark Needham/Envision

A LIVING HERB WREATH

This wreath for the table is as useful as it is beautiful. Start it in the fall, while fresh herb plants are still available in the garden. Low, trailing plants such as thyme and marjoram work better than woody upright plants such as sage.

A double-wire wreath frame

Sphagnum moss

A plate with a rim or a shallow bowl slightly larger than the wreath frame

Herb plants, such as thyme, lemon balm, marjoram, and rosemary

Fill the wreath frame firmly with sphagnum moss and soak overnight in water. Place on the plate or in a shallow bowl. Insert the roots of herb plants, with the soil that clings to them, into the sphagnum at 3-inch intervals. The more trailing herbs you have, the easier it will be to cover the base. Alternate low trailing plants with the more upright ones. Keep evenly moist by pouring water into the center of the dish, and add a few drops of fertilizer with each watering. When any stem becomes straggly, simply weave it back in to cover a bare spot. Misting every week with a sprayer will keep it fresh all winter.

IVY TOPIARY TREE

A live ivy plant can be trained into the shape of a Christmas tree over the course of a few months. Begin with healthy, fairly full plants.

3 small English ivy plants

1 10-inch plastic flowerpot filled with potting soil

Chicken wire cone with a base 8 inches in diameter (see instructions for making a tabletop tree, page 43)

1 12-inch terra-cotta plant pot

Plant the ivy close to the edges of the plastic pot, with the plants equally spaced. Place the wire cone carefully over the pot, pushing the wire very gently into the soil. Pull all the ivy stems to the outside. Entwine the ivy through the wire just enough to hold it so it covers the outside. It will probably not cover the entire cone.

Place the plant in a well-lit window and keep it watered. As the ivy grows, continue to entwine it into the wire frame, winding it around, if necessary, to cover all the bare places. Turn the plant frequently so it grows evenly on all sides. In a few months, the ivy will cover the entire cone, forming a solid green "tree." Display the completed tree in the terra-cotta pot, setting the plastic one inside it. Tie a red bow around the top of the pot during the holidays.

SCENTING YOUR HOME

The very business of decorating and cooking for the holidays—cookies and pies in the oven, fresh balsam, and other greens—adds tempting aromas to your home. But there are ways you can add to these. A simple blend of whole spices simmering on your stove will make everyone think you are baking apple pie: Use a spoonful each of cloves, allspice, and coriander seed with a stick of cinnamon and the peel of a lemon or orange.

If you are making your own balsam wreaths, keep the needles that fall and the tips that break off and put them in a basket with pinecones (preferably those of the white pine, which are pitch-covered). Put the basket on a sunny windowsill, where the warmth will activate the scents. (Don't try to warm these volatile oils near a stove or over a radiator.)

Hot mulled drinks are delicious and scent your home as well.

HOW TO TIE BOWS

The bow is the finishing touch that highlights a wreath. Except for very tiny ones, most bows look more elegant with long tails.

Dried apple slices make a homey wreath.

© Martha McBride/Unicorn Stock Photos

TO TIE A SINGLE BOW:

Tie a double knot around something (a pencil will do), leaving two long ends of equal length. The wider the ribbon, the longer the ends should be. Roughly speaking, each end must be three times the width of the finished bow. Add extra if you want long tails.

Fold the left-hand tail under to make a loop. Bend the loop over across the knot to the right side. Leave your left index finger behind it, between it and the double knot. Your thumb is on top.

Bring the right tail up and over your left thumb and the loop, under your index finger, and back through the space your left thumb is occupying.

With your right index finger, push this loop through until it is big enough to grasp. Hold it and the center band of the bow by closing your right thumb over it. Remove your left hand and use it to grasp the loop, which is now on the left side. Pull the loop through to tighten the knot slightly.

Don't pull it crimped-tight yet, since you may want to tighten or loosen it to make the bow even. You can slip the loops and tails in order to make them the size you want.

When you are satisfied with it, firm the knot by pulling on the back of the left-hand loop and the front of the right-hand loop. That tightens the knot without disturbing the bow. Slip the knot off the pencil and use the little loop on the back as a base for attaching the bow.

A STITCHED BOW:

Cut a long piece of ribbon and determine its center. Fold both ends in and past the center, crossing them at the center and forming two loops the size you want your bow. Cut a short piece of ribbon, fold it over the center to form the "knot," and pull it tight enough to puff the bow and make it look tied. Then simply stitch this ribbon loop in the back, stitching through the crossed ribbon, but not through the front of the knot.

A MULTI-LOOPED BOW:

A way to make a full and less formal bow, perfect for cotton ribbons, is to make a series of loops (like ribbon candy), holding it in the center. Take a long piece of thin, very flexible wire and wind it tightly about the center. As you wind, the ribbon will gather into folds that make the loops stand out. Then all you have to do is separate the loops slightly, and attach two pieces of ribbon for the tails.

A STITCHED BOW

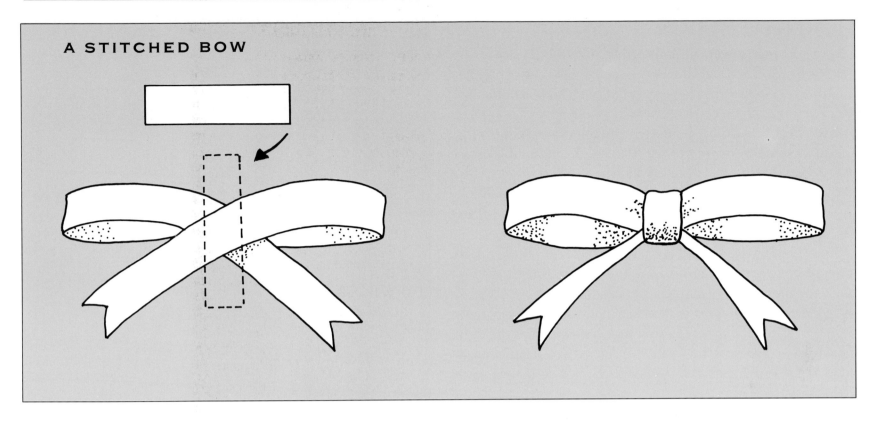

A MULTI-LOOPED BOW

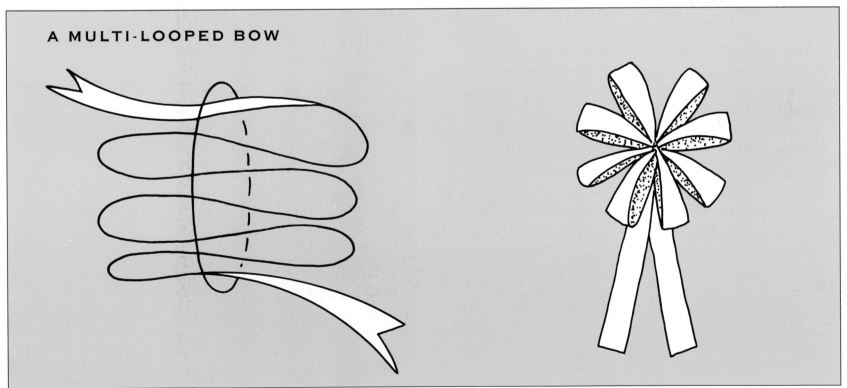

POINSETTIAS

The bright red flowers of poinsettias are actually leaves, not blossoms. The true flower is the cluster at the center of the rosette of red upper leaves. Whatever their technicalities, they are the favorite Christmas plant. Over 25 million of these decorate homes each year during the holidays.

Use them alone or in groups. A cluster of them in a corner of the front hall—one elevated on an upturned flowerpot in the corner and two or three in front of it sitting on the floor—creates a bright accent. Or use a larger grouping in the same way in the corner of a large room.

Since poinsettias should not be in direct sunlight for more than an hour or so a day, a sunny windowsill is not the best place for them. But poinsettias do need light. A good test of the correct natural light is whether a person of normal eyesight can read fine print. If they can, the room has enough light to keep a poinsettia healthy. Water them frequently, whenever the soil feels dry to the touch, but do not let them stand in water.

Contrary to popular myth, the poinsettia is not poisonous. The United States Department of Health and Human Services' Bureau of Product Safety reports that despite numerous reports of children having eaten various parts of the plant, there was no poisoning. Ohio State University conducted laboratory tests and failed to find any evidence of toxicity. While children should not eat any houseplant or Christmas green, the poinsettia is no worse than any other plant and no one seems to know how this rumor started or how it got its dangerous reputation. So the next time you hear that poinsettias are poisonous, you can reply "Bah, humbug," and continue to brighten your Christmas with these beautiful plants.

© Thomas Lindley/FPG International

DECORATE WITH CANDLELIGHT

Candles can be the busy hostess's best friend, for they leave corners in shadow and highlight the places you choose. Show off a collection of candleholders by grouping them on a coffee table or end table with candles of different heights. Protect lit candles in your windows with pierced-tin cylinder-shaped lanterns. The light flickers through, but the flame is covered. Light an entire room with thick candles set inside glass hurricane globes. These reflect and magnify the light while keeping the flame safely covered. Candles protected in this way make a romantic room lighting for a winter party.

Tip: To remove candle wax from fabric, place an ice cube over it, then peel the wax off.

WINDOWSILL GREENS ARRANGEMENTS

Windowsills are the perfect place for sprays of evergreen, but are often too narrow to support a vase. This arrangement uses a long, narrow basket designed to hold crackers, just the right shape for a windowsill.

A long, narrow cracker basket

Oasis® or other floral foam to fit the basket

Toothpicks or wooden skewers

A sheet of plastic wrap large enough to line the basket

Assorted evergreen sprigs, such as white pine, balsam, spruce, juniper, cedar, and boxwood

Red berries such as bittersweet or sumac, or rose hips

Soak the Oasis® in water and let it drain. Line the basket with plastic wrap and put the Oasis® in it. Secure at the ends and edges with toothpicks or skewers, pushing them through the holes in the basket and into the Oasis®. Put these skewers near the top rim of the basket so they will not puncture the bottom of the plastic.

Begin with the larger sprigs and push their stems into the basket near the center of the back. Continue to work to the edges, inserting the stems at more and more of an angle until the final sprigs drape over the sides onto the work surface. Soft, flexible greens such as white pine are best for these edges, since they drape gracefully. When the back layer is full, defining the shape of the arrangement, fill in the center and front with shorter sprigs, mixing them for variety. Add accents of holly or other red berries if they are available. Fresh flowers may be added to this arrangement, since the Oasis® will be kept moist. Red or white carnations, small red roses, or white mums provide a nice contrast to the dark greens.

Water the arrangement frequently but lightly, keeping the Oasis® moist at all times, but not enough to allow water to leak through the plastic.

A TABLETOP TREE

Finding a small tree for the center of a table or a buffet is not as easy as it may seem. Real trees rarely achieve that perfect a shape: That comes with age and shearing. Most of the tabletop trees sold at Christmas tree farms are really the tips of larger trees. Even these are sometimes a little bare.

They do allow a lot of space for ornaments, but if you prefer a fuller, perfectly shaped centerpiece tree, the best way to get it is to make your own. Unlike a natural tree, your manmade tree can have a variety of greens and can be any size. For an unusual and fragrant tree, try creating it from branches of rosemary.

1 piece of small-gauge chicken wire, 18 by 36 inches

Wire cutters

Florist's tape

Sphagnum or other floral moss

Branches of white pine, cedar, boxwood, rosemary, or other fairly flexible evergreens

Cut the chicken wire screening into a semicircle with wire cutters. Fold the straight side in half to form a cone, overlapping more for a narrower tree and less for a wider one. Twist the cut wire ends into the mesh to fasten the edge and hold the cone in shape.

Wrap the bottom edge with florist's tape, stretching the tape as you work to make it stick. Check the tree to be sure it stands straight. If it does not, you can pull it into shape or fold up a little wire on the longer side. Soak sphagnum moss in water and drain so it is moist but not dripping. Fill the cone lightly with the wet moss and set the tree on a platter or a round tray.

Beginning at the bottom, push short lengths of evergreens into the cone, with their stems pointing upward inside the cone and the tips curving downward like the branches of a fir tree. Continue working up the sides of the cone, using slightly shorter stems as you work. At the top, you will run out of space inside.

Choose one straight sprig and push it straight down into the point of the cone to form the tip of the tree. With very short sprigs, fill in the top of the tree, pushing the evergreens in so they face outward and upward. Heavily branched sprigs that cover a lot of surface without many stems are best for this part. If there are places you simply cannot cover, you can fill them in with small ornaments, but you can usually manage to cover the top neatly by forcing stems into the wire.

Keep the moss moist by turning the tree over very carefully whenever it seems dry and pouring water through it. Let it drain lying on its side and stand it up again. If you have ornaments on the tree, you can water it by pouring a thin stream of water from a sharp-spouted watering can into the very top of the tree and letting it drip through. Even without water, the tree will last for several weeks.

LET GIFTS DECORATE YOUR HOME

Wrap gifts well ahead of Christmas and pile them in brightly colored arrangements beside the fireplace, along the mantel, on a hall table, in the center of a coffee table, or in any other space that could use a little Christmas cheer. Small or oddly shaped packages can be grouped in baskets.

If you have a lot of guests during the holidays, wrap jars of homemade preserves in bright red and green tissue and twist the ends like firecrackers. Pile these in a basket near the door and present them to guests as they leave. Any other small item can be wrapped and kept near the door for that moment when a gift is needed unexpectedly. Meanwhile, they make a colorful decoration.

DRESS UP YOUR HOLIDAY TABLE

To make informal holiday tablecloths, stitch together two lengths of Christmas print calico. The busy design will hide the seam. For an elegant dinner, gift wrap your table by crossing two lengths of wide red ribbon at the center over a white tablecloth to make it look like a package. The ribbons should drape down the sides to the edges of the tablecloth. To complete the effect, use a giant red bow at the cross as a centerpiece.

Pile colorful glass Christmas tree ornaments in a crystal bowl for a centerpiece and tuck tiny sprigs of pine between them. Decorate a basket of red apples in the same way.

Roll your napkins and tie a ribbon around each as a napkin ring, finishing it off with a bow. Tie bows around the stems of water glasses. Make little bouquets of evergreen tied with red ribbon and place above the plate at each setting. Carry out the theme with a low bowl of greens as a centerpiece.

CHAPTER THREE

CHRISTMAS TREES

Everyone has a favorite Christmas tree. The most popular is the **balsam**. It looks and smells like the quintessential Christmas tree and is easy to decorate, being neither bushy nor prickly. Best of all, you can strip the tree of its needles after Christmas and use them for balsam sachets and pillows. Also fragrant is the **Douglas fir**, a native of the Rocky Mountains and Northwest. The **Fraser fir** grows in the Southeast and looks much like the balsam.

Spruce also has a classic Christmas tree shape, though it tends to be fuller than balsam. This makes it difficult to decorate with large ornaments that need to be placed farther into the tree rather than on the ends of branches. But if you favor smaller ornaments and garlands (popcorn strings, tinsel, and the like), a spruce tree is just right.

In shape, the **Scotch pine** is more spherical than conical, and its branches are so thickly furred with spiny needles that it is nearly impossible to put lights or ornaments deep into its foliage. In addition, it scratches.

CHOOSING AND CARING FOR YOUR CHRISTMAS TREE

If you are buying a tree that has already been cut, remember that a fresh tree not only lasts longer but is safer and less prone to combustion. If it is possible, get a recently cut tree. When shaken, the tree should lose few, if any, needles. If you can easily bend a needle without breaking it between two fingers, then the tree is likely to be fresh. Storing an early-bought tree in water until Christmas is much better than buying a dry one later.

Be sure to measure from floor to ceiling before you choose a tree. Surrounded by its giant neighbors, a tree looks much smaller in the woods or tree lot than it will in your living room. Also, think where you will put the tree and look at it from all sides. If it is to go in a fairly small room, you might look for a tall, thin tree. If it is to sit right against a wall, try to find an otherwise perfect tree with one flat side.

Cut your tree as late in the season as possible and keep its base in water at all times. Cut the trunk at a slight angle so it will have a larger absorption area. When you are ready to put the tree in the stand, cut it straight so it will stand better. Use a firm stand with a large water basin. If you purchase a tree that's already cut, immediately saw a piece off the base to give it a fresh start, and keep it in water. To prolong the "life" of any tree, put it in hot water to begin with; thereafter, tap water can be used to keep the basin filled.

Your tree stand should be wide enough at the base so that the tree cannot easily tip over. This is especially important if you have small children or pets. If your floor is thickly carpeted, it is wise to put a large sheet of plywood or other firm material under the tree stand to stabilize it.

A living Christmas tree has many advantages and requires little care while you have it in the house. The ball of roots should be put in a plate or shallow bowl that's deep enough so dirt or water won't spill on the floor or rug. Place the tree away from any sources of heat and be sure it stays cool. Keep the ball moist, but don't soak it. Keep the room well ventilated and let in plenty of light to keep it in good condition until you plant it outside. Observe the safety precautions as if it were a cut tree. Even though live trees' needles are not as likely to catch fire, it is still a good idea to be careful.

When Christmas is over, take all the ornaments, tinsel, and other decorations off the tree. Pick a spot in the yard where your tree can grow without interference. Don't pick a place too close to wires or to the house, because the tree will need plenty of room to grow and spread out. If you cannot replant your tree it can be used as kindling for a wood stove or fireplace, but not as firewood, since its needles will cause too many sparks if used in large quantities.

TRIMMING THE TREE

Second only to opening presents, trimming the tree is a highlight of the Christmas season. It is a time of renewal and of memories as all the familiar ornaments are unpacked, each one a piece of some Christmas past.

While every family seems to have its own ritual for trimming the tree, there is a vague order of business that makes it easier. The tree should be set up at least a few hours before you are ready to trim. This gives it a chance to warm up, stretch, and have its limbs fall to their natural levels.

Because it is difficult to place lights on a tree hung with ornaments, the lights should go on first. The lights' heavy cord helps weigh down or hold up branches to fill in bare spots. If you use tiny lights they will balance easily since there are so many, but larger lights may need quite a lot of moving about to keep them from all being in one place. Look at the tree from every angle to make sure they are well positioned.

Although some (tall) people manage to "crown" their tree with a star as a grand finale, practicality suggests that on a large tree with fragile ornaments, crowning is best done right after the lights.

If you are hanging garlands or chains, they should come next. Your garlands may be tinsel, chains, strings of beads, candy, popcorn, or cranberries. Professional decorators who do those perfect trees in store windows have a few tricks with garlands that help bring the tree together and frame the other ornaments. Begin draping garlands on the bottom branches and loop a heavy garland once around each branch that supports it. Leave plenty of drape—you don't want the garland to appear to tie the tree up like a bundle. Hang your largest and showiest ornaments in the places where garlands intersect and frame smaller ornaments in the spaces between. Plain glass balls should hang inside the branches, near the trunk, to reflect lights and give depth to the tree.

Hang the smallest ornaments at the very tips of branches where they can be seen. Or have a separate tabletop tree for these tiny treasures.

© Cezus/FPG International

TREE TRIMS TO MAKE

CALICO HEARTS

Bright old-fashioned prints, especially in Christmas colors and designs, bring a traditional look to the Christmas tree. These hearts may also be hung in windows or be made in different sizes. Add whole spices or potpourri to the filling for fragrance.

Calico scraps at least 5 inches square

½ yard narrow, gathered, lace trim

Cotton or fiberfill for stuffing

½ yard narrow grosgrain ribbon in a matching or complementary color

Cut two hearts from calico fabric, using the pattern provided. Stitch lace around the outer edge of one heart, ¼ inch from the edge. Stitch it to the right side of the fabric, with the ruffle facing in.

Place second heart face down over the first, over the lace, so that right sides are facing and the edges of the two hearts match. Pin in two or three places to secure. Turn hearts over and stitch around the edge, following the first line of stitches exactly. This assures that the lace will show evenly when the hearts are turned right side out. Leave a 2-inch space unstitched along one straight edge.

Turn to the right side, pushing with your fingers to smooth the edges under the lace. Fill with stuffing and blind-stitch to close the seam.

Cut a 5-inch length of ribbon and fold it to make two loops with ends meeting in the center (*see diagram, page 114*). Secure ends with one or two stitches, leaving thread attached. Wrap one end of the remaining ribbon around the center to look like the tie on a bow; secure with a stitch, but do not cut. Fold loose end into a 3-inch hanging loop, cutting off remaining ribbon. Secure the ribbon to the heart with a few stitches; knot and end thread.

YARN DOLLS

These old-fashioned ornaments are fun for children to make, but adults will enjoy them, too. You can add felt clothing and accessories and dress them as characters such as Little Red Riding Hood, elves, Mrs. Santa, a snowman, or Robin Hood.

Yarn ends in single or mixed colors and textures

Stiff cardboard, 3 by 4 inches

Scraps of felt for trim

Cut a 12-inch piece of strong yarn for a tie and lay it along the 3-inch edge of the cardboard. Wrap yarn along the wide side of the cardboard, at right angles to the tie, wrapping right over the 12-inch piece of yarn (*see diagram, page 115*). The number of wraps necessary will depend on the size of the yarn. Fine, baby-weight yarns will require much more than thicker, bulky yarns. You will know when you have enough to make a full doll, but remember that only half of the yarn shows as you wrap.

Make the tie into a single knot to hold the yarn together, and cut the yarn along the edge opposite the tie. Be careful not to let the pieces fall apart as you cut. Pull the knot tight and secure with a second one. The yarn will look like a loose tassel.

Tie the neck tightly, about 1 inch below the top. If there is not enough yarn to make a good round head, move the neck up. You can trim the bottom of the doll later to keep it in scale.

Wrap the yarn around the short side of the card to make arms. Use about one-quarter as much as you did for the body. Carefully slip this little hank of yarn off the cardboard, holding it together. Tie the wrists about ¼ to ½ inch from each end.

Divide the yarn just below the neck into two groups and place the arms between these. Tie again around the waist. If the doll is to be a boy, split the yarn for legs and tie at the ankles. Tie the top yarn ends together to form a hanging loop, trim the bottom even, and push the ends from the neck and wrist ties into the yarn to hide them.

You can add to this basic doll by cutting a circle of pink felt and drawing a face on it with colored pencils. Or you can make pointed hats from semicircles of felt or dress them in capes or jerkins.

These dolls are particularly attractive when made in natural, dyed, homespun wools. Their soft colors and uneven textures add interest to the dolls. These dolls are at their best without any added felt accessories.

WOVEN STRAW ORNAMENT

Straw weaving and the creation of symbolic and decorative figures from wheat and other grains has its origin far back in primitive times. Wherever wheat or suitable straw is grown—in Mexico, in Central Europe, in the midwestern United States—country people still make these lovely harvest decorations.

Heads of wheat or barley, with long stems (well dried)

Stout thread in straw color

A large pan or bowl of warm water

Old scissors (not good fabric scissors)

A terry-cloth towel

12-inch lengths of ½-inch ribbon

Cut wheat stalks just above the first joint so that you have heads with long, perfectly smooth stems attached.

Soak straw for twenty minutes in lukewarm water. Remove a piece and bend it gently; if it is pliable and does not crack, it is ready to use. If not, return it to the water for ten more minutes. When straw is ready, wrap it in a terry-cloth towel and leave for fifteen minutes. Remove only as much as you need to work with and leave the rest in the towel. Any straw left over should be spread out to dry so it will not mildew.

Choose eight well-matched heads with long stems; leave four in the towel and work with the other four. With the thread, tie together just below the heads.

Turn the bundle so that heads face down and the stems (straws) are face up. Spread the straws out to form a cross and hold flat with your left thumb (reverse this if you are left-handed). With one arm of the cross pointing directly toward you (we will call this the bottom straw), bend the top straw toward you, folding it flat so it lies parallel to the bottom one. Fold the bottom one upward to the top position. Press both flat and repeat this process with the left and right straws.

Continue this sequence of first one and then the other set of straws until the braid is 4 to 5 inches long. Tie the end with thread and return the braid to the towel.

Repeat with the other four long straws.

Cut three more straws to equal lengths, about 6 to 7 inches long below the heads.

Tie the ends of the two plaited sections to the center of the bundle of three straws, with the heads of the braided pieces facing upward and the other heads facing down. Bend the braids over and tie them again where the thread holds them just below the heads. This will form a heart shape, with all the heads in a spray at its base. Include in the tie all those straws from the braid that are long enough to reach. Cut short ones just below the first tie.

Tie the ribbon at the base of the heart, just above the heads, forming a neat bow. Evenly trim the ribbon ends.

Put the finished ornament in an airy place to dry completely.

Miniature wreaths can be used on a tree, to decorate presents, or stand on their own.

MINIATURE CANE WREATHS

Miniature wreath bases of entwined cane or vines can be purchased in craft and hobby stores. There is almost no end to the ways in which you can decorate these for tree ornaments.

Miniature cane or vine wreath base

Narrow red ribbon

Small wooden hearts, ribbon roses, flocked animals, or other decorations

Quick-drying glue or glue gun

Wrap the ribbon around the wreath in a spiral and tie into a bow at the top. Make a small loop of ribbon for hanging at the back of the wreath behind the bow.

Glue hearts or animals to the wreath, placing these over the ribbon and arranging them in a balanced design. If you are using the ribbon roses, put them in groups of three.

These are good ornaments to mail as small gifts or package decorations, since they are fairly sturdy.

© Jennifer Lévy

BEESWAX ORNAMENTS

Nothing adds warmth to a tree like the honey tones of beeswax. These are especially nice in the shape of teddy bears.

Beeswax

Double boiler for melting

*Plastic candy molds in
    appropriate shapes:
    bears, animals, stars,
    etc.*

Narrow red satin ribbon

Melt wax in the double boiler over low heat. A metal pitcher suspended in a pot of boiling water is even easier to use, since it has a pour-spout. Cut ribbon into 3-inch lengths.

Carefully pour melted wax into the plastic molds. Quickly imbed the ends of a ribbon in the top of each one as a hanger. Place molds in the freezer, taking care to keep them level. In a few minutes they will be firm enough to pop out, so you can reuse the mold.

Be sure to store these in a cool area, since they will melt if kept in a hot place.

Molds are available in many holiday designs.

© Christopher C. Bain

MILKWEED POD STAR

Crown your tree with a star made from one of nature's most common weeds. These can be sprayed gold for a more elegant effect, but many prefer to leave them in their natural state.

5 milkweed pods of equal sizes and similar shapes

A perfect yellow strawflower or other round, dried flower or seed pod

Quick-drying glue or glue gun

Medium-gauge florist's wire

Arrange milkweed pods in a star shape. Using very little glue, attach them at the edges and center. Run a loop of wire through the center, leaving long tails on the back for attaching to the tree. Glue the strawflower in the exact center of the star. You can add rays between the points using straw or the strong, straight stems of grasses.

WALNUT SHELL LAMBS

Make a whole flock of these lambs to gambol in groups across your tree, or use them to decorate wreaths.

Walnut shell halves

White acrylic or oil paint

Black felt

Quick-drying glue

Nylon or other invisible thread for hangers

Paint walnut shells white and allow them to dry thoroughly. Meanwhile, cut feet, heads, and tails from black felt, using patterns. You will need two feet, one head, and one tail for each two half shells.

When the shells are dry, lay half of them, split side up, on the work surface and glue heads, tails, feet, and hangers (*see diagram, page 114*) to the flat edge of the shell. When the glue has set enough to keep the felt from slipping, glue the second set of halves over the first. The halves do not have to match perfectly, but should be the same size.

Allow the glue to dry thoroughly before hanging.

COUNTRY DECORATIONS

Nowhere is the warm, homespun style of country decorating more appropriate than in a home decked in its Christmas finery. Warm colors and designs drawn from the farm, nature, and folk art give any home, however small or urban, the look and feel of a gracious country home.

There are so many crafts you can do to make your Christmas a country Christmas. Again, the projects included in this chapter should just be the starting point. Take ideas from the things around you and from things you have seen elsewhere. Nearly anything you see can be made your own—to become a tradition in your home.

Miniature trees with a food theme make perfect table centerpieces.

COOKIE TREE

This decoration is traditional in Scandinavia, where it is hung with spicy cookies. But it can be used to display special ornaments, gingerbread boys, or other treasures of the holiday season.

A *block of wood, at least 6 inches square and ½ inch thick*

1 ½-inch dowel, 18 inches long

¼-inch dowels, one each: 12 inches, 9 inches, and 6 inches long

Drill with ½-inch bit

Glue gun

Red cord

Sandpaper

Measure the exact center of the block and drill a hole through it. Be sure the hole is perfectly straight. Smooth the edge of the hole and the corners of the wood with sandpaper.

Smooth the ends of all the dowels with sandpaper. Lay the large dowel flat on the work surface and lay the smaller ones across it, 4 inches apart, beginning 4 inches from one end with the longest ¼-inch dowel and ending 2 inches from the other with the 6-inch dowel. They should be centered exactly on the big dowel "stem" and should be at perfect right angles to it. Glue these in place, using the glue gun. A little glue will show, but this will be covered with the red cord.

Wrap each of the intersections with a cross of red cord, tying it firmly and trimming the ends close. Put a drop of glue into the hole in the block of wood and put the end of the tree stem in the hole. Be sure it is straight.

These trees are often decorated with fresh red apples impaled on the ends of the dowels. Artificial apples can be glued there, or bright red beads can be glued to the ends. Or, they may be left plain. Make decorative cookies (see index for recipes) with holes in the tops and hang them on the tree using the red cord.

PAPER CUTOUTS

Taking a hint from the strings of paper dolls children often make, these paper cutouts are a simpler version of the delicate and detailed paper cuttings made in Switzerland and Germany. They add a festive touch to door frames, mantels, and cabinets. Or use them as the Pennsylvania Dutch do, to line the edges of shelves.

A variety of papers can be used: parchment for a slightly more formal look or brown paper grocery bags for cutouts that are the color of gingerbread boys.

Brown paper bags or parchment paper

Sharp paper scissors

White tempera or acrylic paint (optional, for brown paper)

Measure a length of paper to fit the area you wish to decorate. You may need to do several strips and tape them together for longer spaces. The width of the paper will depend on the size of the design, but for the gingerbread boy shown (*see diagram, page 115*), it should be about 4 inches wide.

Fold the strip of paper accordian style, leaving ½ inch extra on either end if several pieces will have to be joined together. The width of the fold will also depend on the size of the design, but 3 inches will make the gingerbread boys.

Fold the stack of paper in half lengthwise, or, if this will make it too thick to cut, omit this last fold. If you are unsure of your freehand cutting, trace half the design onto the folded paper as shown (or the whole design if the paper was too thick to fold again). Cut through all thicknesses and unfold. It is sometimes necessary to trim the edges of the figures at one end of the string, since they become fatter toward the outside of the fold.

Press the paper so it will lie flat or, if you are making short strings to go on bookcases or cabinet doors, you can leave them in their accordian shape to stand up.

If you have used brown paper, you can add little dots of white paint to look like frosting, making eyes and buttons down the front, even a little bow tie at the neck.

GINGERBREAD VILLAGE

Even five- and six-year-olds can master the construction of simple gingerbread houses made from graham crackers, with the help of a few extra adult hands. Ages seven and up will need considerably less help.

Cardboard for a base, about 8 by 11 inches

Small candy canes, Necco® wafers (for the slate roof), gumdrops, candy mint leaves, peppermint drops, licorice sticks, miniature marshmallows, and other small candies

Graham crackers

Royal icing

Note: When you are working with the icing, put a small amount out in a small dish and keep the rest tightly covered, since it dries out quickly. Also, each house requires eight squares of graham cracker, but you will want to allow plenty of extras in case some break.

Using a sharp knife, separate one of the crackers along the center scored line to make two squares; this will assure that they break evenly.

Lay one double cracker flat near the center of the cardboard. Spread frosting along two opposite edges and stand another whole cracker at each edge, outside the base cracker, so that their edges are standing on the cardboard. Hold or prop them upright for a couple of minutes until the frosting is stiff. Be sure they are straight.

Spread frosting on three edges of one of the half (square) crackers and carefully place it *inside* the two standing walls, with its bottom on top of the base. It should fit just inside the two end walls, and will stand a tiny bit higher. Allow a minute or two for this frosting to set, before repeating this with the fourth wall. Your house should now be able to stand up by itself.

Cut a cracker diagonally with a very sharp knife, first perforating it in a straight line. If the crackers are very brittle, hold them over a pan of boiling water to soften them slightly before cutting.

Spread frosting along the long (cut) edge, and carefully stand the triangle on the top of one end wall. You will have to hold this in place until it is dry. Repeat with the other end wall.

Frost three edges of a whole (rectangular) cracker and lay in place on the top of the house. Repeat with a second cracker to complete the roof.

Wait about twenty minutes before starting to decorate the house. Frost the roof and then lay rows of Necco® wafer "slates" beginning at the bottom edge and overlapping slightly with each row. Or simply cover the roof with icing snow. Add a broken piece of candy cane for a chimney, or build one out of small squares of cracker.

Entryways or even front porches can be added with candy-stick pillars. Licorice laces, clipped into short lengths with scissors, are perfect for outlining windows and doors. Gumdrops or peppermint drops lined along the ridge pole help to define the shape of the roof, and the rounded tops of candy canes are splendid fan windows over front doors.

When the house is finished, spread a light coating of frosting snow around the base and make a front walk from Necco® wafers or flat mints. You can landscape the yard with trees made of spearmint candy leaves or large marshmallows, which look like snow-covered shrubbery. A candy-cane lamppost might add just the right touch for the front yard.

You can make a whole village of these houses for a mantel or tabletop arrangement, varying their size, decor, and landscaping. Make smaller houses by using single (square) crackers for side as well as end walls. Doghouses can be made by cutting these squares into fourths (easier if you steam the crackers briefly). Once you have mastered cutting, you can even make barns with hip roofs.

ROYAL ICING

3 egg whites

1 pound confectioner's sugar, sifted

1 teaspoon vanilla

½ teaspoon cream of tartar

Combine all ingredients in a mixing bowl and beat with an electric mixer until the frosting is stiff. This may take up to ten minutes. Keep frosting in a covered container or at least covered with a damp towel, since it dries very quickly.

Makes 3 cups.

CORN HUSK DOLLS

One of the earliest of American craft materials, corn husks were used by Native Americans to make dolls and baskets. They taught these skills to the early settlers, who also made doormats from the husks.

Make corn husk dolls in a variety of sizes. Small ones are good tree decorations and package ornaments.

PREPARING CORN HUSKS FOR CRAFT USES

You don't have to live in the country to make these dolls. Fresh corn on the cob from the grocery store provides enough husks for this project. You can dry the husks yourself by cutting the stem end off the corn, close to the point where the kernels begin. Slip the husks off, discarding the tough, coarse, dark green outside husks. Spread the softer inside husks on a screen or newspapers to dry. They will do this faster in the sun, but a shady place will do very well, too. If you dry them outdoors, be sure to bring them in at night. When the husks are stiff and crisp, you are ready to make your dolls. Do not try to use the husks fresh from the corn. They must dry and then be softened in water before they can be used in crafts without curling and twisting, which would ruin your dolls.

12 to 15 dried cornhusks

A bowl of warm water, large enough to hold the husks

Sturdy white or beige thread or raffia

Scissors

Soak the husks in water for about ten minutes. Take them out only as you need them, leaving the others in the water.

Stack five or six long husks with all the narrow ends at the top and tie them into a bundle, about 2 inches from the top.

Roll the narrow ends down in a tight roll, as far as the place where you have tied them. Turn the husks so this part is at the bottom and hold this roll between your left thumb and index finger.

Pull the husks, one by one, down over the rolled part, as if you were peeling a banana. Catch each one under your left thumb as it is pulled down. They should be as smooth and tight as you can get them, and spread around the rolled husks from side to side. Tie the husks again, right under the lump formed by the rolled husks, to form a neck.

To make the arms, take three narrow husks (or split

© Christopher C. Bain

Take one perfect, wide husk and lay it, wide side up, over the front of the doll, so that the widest end is over the face and the pointed end is about halfway down the skirt. Tie once more around the waist, securing this husk over the rest. Pull the husk down and smooth it over the skirt to make an apron.

Trim the skirt evenly so the doll will stand, and trim the arms to a natural length.

While the doll is still wet, you can shape the arms to hold something or turn them up or down. Tie them in the position you like. After the doll is completely dry (overnight, at least), cut these threads away and the arms will remain in place. You may have to trim the skirt again slightly after the husks are dry.

The dolls' heads may be covered with scarves made from triangles of husk, and bonnets can be made by folding a rectangular husk over the top of the head and folding it like the ends of a package wrapping in back. Hold the bonnet in place by tying it with thread. When the husks are dry, the bonnet will hold its shape and can be held in place with a drop of white glue.

Corn husk dolls traditionally had no faces drawn on them, but there is no reason why you can't add more detail to yours. Be sure the doll is completely dry and use colored pencils to draw the face. Ink will spread, so don't use either markers or paints.

wider ones by pulling them apart lengthwise) and tie them together at one end. Braid these and tie at the other end. Or, you can take a wider husk and roll it into a long pencil shape and tie in the center to hold it together.

Hold the doll facing you— the smoothest side of the head will be the face—and lift the two top husks away from the others. Push the rolled or braided arms right up against the tied neck, under these two husks and fold them back

down over the arms. Tie just below these to form a waist.

With another narrow husk, make a shawl over the doll's shoulders and bring the ends down, crossing them in front at the waist. Tie the waist again.

CONE WREATHS

The varying shades of brown and the unusual textures of cones and seed pods give the wreathmaker the opportunity to create any number of original arrangements. A cone wreath can be exuberant or restrained. It can be any size, depending on the size of the cones and seeds available. And, unlike evergreen boughs, pinecones can be purchased by mail if they do not grow locally.

While it is not essential, many people are more comfortable storing these seeds and cones in their home after they have been baked in a slow oven to kill any insects that might be harbored there. In the case of the white pinecone, which tends to be covered with spots of pitch, baking melts the pitch and evens the color.

Wreathmakers strongly disagree on whether it is better to wire or to glue the cones on. Traditionalists use wire, but many people are perfectly happy with glue now that the glue gun has been created. Whatever method you choose to use, it must allow for the significant movement of the cones due to changes in humidity. Cones continually open and close enough to break the bond of any but a flexible glue. Also, if you choose to use a glue gun, be very careful not to leave any glue showing, and to cut off all the little threads of glue that form when the gun is moved from one place to another.

Some seeds and nuts are almost impossible to wire to a wreath without drilling, so even if you wire the basic wreath you might want to use glue to attach the final pieces.

A double-wire wreath frame

Fine florist's wire

Scissors

A glue gun

A quantity of white pine or blue spruce cones

An assortment of other cones and seeds of various sizes

Soak the white pine or spruce cones in warm water for a few minutes until they close. Wearing gloves or using a cloth to protect your hands, push these larger cones between the upper and lower layers of wire on the wreath frame. You can either have them all facing out or you can alternate. If they all face out, the outer edge of the wreath will look more solid. But if you alternate, you can fill in the spaces with other cones for a less regular effect.

Allow the cones to dry overnight or put the wreath in a slow oven until they dry and open (about an hour). While you are doing this, wire the other cones, preparing a selection of several different kinds.

Beginning with the larger cones, attach them along the center, covering the wires of the wreath frame completely. Push the wire tails through the wreath and twist them together at the back, securing each cone tightly.

Don't cut these wire tails until you are finished. This allows you to find them again if you decide to rearrange the cones, and it also gives you spare wire for fastening the other cones.

One of the major advantages of the wired wreath is that you can move cones around after they are in place by simply untwisting the wires. Experiment with different arrangements of the larger cones, since these will set the tone of your wreath.

Fill in the spaces with the next smaller cones and seeds, ending with hemlock cones and other tiny ones to fill in any space where wire or frame shows. These should be glued in place by touching the stem end to the point of a hot glue gun. It is better to put the glue on the seed and then the seed on the wreath than to try to get a dot of hot glue onto the wreath.

ATTACHING WIRES TO CONES

Since wires for attaching cones to the wreath must be flexible enough to hide inside the cones as well as tie and twist easily, a fairly fine wire is the best. Cut it in lengths of 8 and 12 inches, the longer ones for larger cones.

Slip the middle of a piece of wire under the top row of petals (scales) on a cone and pull it tightly. Twist the ends together, securely, so the wire does not slip. There should be two tails of nearly equal length. By placing the wires under the top line of petals, the tails can be pulled up toward the stem to attach the cone so it points directly up, or it can be left to come out the side so it attaches flat.

© Lynn Karlin

POMANDERS

The sweet, spicy fragrance of pomanders lasts for years and blends perfectly with the other scents of Christmas. While they can be made of different fruits, small, firm apples are the easiest to work with and last the longest. Or try crab apples or kumquats, and use them for tree ornaments. Pomanders piled in a bowl or basket are as pretty to look at as they are to sniff. Or combine them with large pinecones in a basket.

Firm apples

Whole cloves

Wire hairpins

A terry-cloth towel

Working over a towel to protect surfaces from juice, fill the entire surface of the apple with cloves. Leave ⅛ to ¹/₁₆ of an inch between cloves to allow for the apple's shrinkage as it dries. Leave the inner part of the stem area open, since it will shrink down, too.

Push the wire hairpin into the stem end of the apple, leaving enough of a loop to tie a ribbon through. Put on string or wire loops and hang to dry, or place on a plate in a dry place. Each day, gently roll the pomanders in your palms, pressing in the cloves that have loosened and keeping the pomanders in a nice round shape.

When they are completely dry, tie ribbon bows through the hairpin loop.

Often, you will see instructions for rolling the pomanders in a combination of powdered spices and orrisroot, but this is unnecessary and makes them unsightly and messy. The orrisroot causes many people discomfort and bits of spice continue to fall off. To contain these, the pomanders are often wrapped in net that is not nearly as attractive as a rich, brown, clove-studded ball. Rolling in spices does not extend their life; they will last many years without this and can be refreshed if necessary by swishing them in a bowl of warm water, shaking them off, and hanging them to dry. This is also a good way to remove dust if they have been out in the open for some time.

A BASKET OF VELVET FRUITS

The bright colors and soft texture of velvet makes this permanent fruit basket appropriate for any room of the house, but it is a favorite on the dining room table. For the kitchen, use bright calico prints.

Small scraps of velvet, velveteen, or velour fabrics in red, yellow, and orange

Green felt scraps

Cotton or fiberfill for stuffing

Yellow embroidery thread

Cut pattern pieces (*see diagram, page 116*) in appropriate colors and assemble as follows:

Strawberry: On the right side of the fabric make tiny yellow stitches at random to look like seeds. Fold in half with the right sides together and stitch along straight side. Turn, stuff, and gather top to close (it does not have to close completely). Cut a hull from felt and stitch over the top. The strawberries may be used for tree ornaments, in which case add a loop of narrow green ribbon for hanging.

Pear: Stitch the four pieces together along the sides, with right sides facing. Turn, stuff, and gather bottom edge loosely. Turn under the edges on the circle and blind stitch over the bottom to cover the opening. Add a felt leaf at the top.

Orange: Stitch all four pieces together to form a circle, leaving a space for stuffing in one side. Turn and fill, then blind stitch the opening. Add a felt leaf at the top.

Apple: Stitch and stuff as for the orange. Using a stout thread and a long needle, stitch through the center of the apple, from the point where all the seams meet on the top to the point where they meet on the bottom. Pull tight to make a dent in the top of the apple and tie firmly. Add a felt leaf at the top.

To make a large basket of fruit, you will want to add grapes, which can be made from 3-inch circles of purple velvet gathered around the edge, stuffed, and pulled tight. Gather these into groups resembling bunches of grapes and stitch them together so that all the gathered edges are on the inside where they don't show.

CINNAMON SWAGS

Long sticks of fragrant cinnamon tied with ribbon and decorated with cones and greens make attractive centerpieces for a buffet or small table. Their long, narrow shape also makes them perfect for windowsills or mantelpieces.

10 to 12 cinnamon sticks, at least 10 inches long

Sprigs of dried flowers in deep reds, such as plumed celosia or clusters of sumac berries

Pinecones

Florist's wire

Taffeta ribbon, 1 to 2 inches wide, in deep red or red-and-green plaid

Tie the bundle of cinnamon sticks together at the center, using the florist's wire. Spread the sticks a little so they are not in a tight clump at the ends.

Attach wires to the pinecones (see page 72) and set aside. Wire the dried flowers or sumac to longer stems, if necessary. Tie the ribbon around the center of the cinnamon, covering the wire, and tie a large bow. If the bow looks skimpy (no two bundles of cinnamon will be the same size), add a wire-wrapped double bow (see page 36), tucking it under the tied bow and tying the wires behind. Add decorative sprigs of dried flowers, pinecones, even sprays of evergreen to complete the arrangement.

THE FINE ART OF GIVING

Giving gifts is one of the oldest Christmas traditions, beginning with the arrival of the three Wise Men at the first Christmas. Choosing gifts for family and friends can either be a chore or it can be part of the fun of the holidays. For many people, the crowded stores and traffic snarls are not a treasured part of the holidays; it is here that another country tradition solves a great part of the problem. From the days of the first Sears Roebuck catalog, people who lived in rural areas have ordered things by mail. Catalog shopping has now become common to people all over, and it is still one of the best ways to find really unusual gifts and decorations. But you have to know which catalogs to shop from.

The usual run of gift catalogs begin to look very much alike after a while—full of gimmicks and plastic do-dads that grow more expensive each year. Clever shoppers begin to look in the less common places for quality country gifts. There are several kinds of catalogs that are not sent in a mass mailing to everyone whose name appears on a list. Small mail-order companies, often family-run cottage industries or craftsmen's cooperatives, send catalogs only to those who ask for them, often charging a modest fee to cover the printing and mailing. But for a dollar or two, you can save hours of time and gallons of gasoline, and find interesting gifts that your friends won't have seen before.

Museum shops are an especially nice place to shop before the holidays. If you have a large museum or reconstructed historical site near you, these shops offer beautiful and carefully selected gifts. Many smaller restorations have modest brochures describing some of their offerings, and nearly all of them specialize in historic replicas and hand-

Brightly wrapped Christmas gifts can decorate your home.

made items. Along with finding gifts that are interesting, beautiful, and unusual, you will have the satisfaction of knowing that the profit from these shops goes into the museum's treasury to acquire new collections and protect and preserve the treasures they have. It is really like giving two gifts in one.

Another catalog that nearly always offers gifts that you would never find elsewhere comes from the many small herb businesses throughout the United States and Canada. These are usually small, family-run farms, with modest catalogs and very personal response to their customers. The gifts they offer are designed right there, made by family members and friends. Instead of mass-produced wreaths, theirs will be one-of-a-kind, often made to order. Bouquets of dried flowers, pottery balls filled with potpourri, gift baskets of packets of farm-grown herbs, and the personal favorite herb blends of each family fill these catalogs.

Hartman's Herb Farm in Massachusetts offers a lovely herbal calendar designed and drawn by Lynn Hartman. Betsy Williams, also in Massachusetts, creates beautiful wreaths of herbs and dried flowers (hers is one of the few of these catalogs that has full-color photographs). Rosemary House in Pennsylvania has a large selection of herb-related gifts, plus recipe collections based on years of experimenting with these delicious flavors.

Other herb farms offer "gifts that give twice." Instructional booklets on gardening and herb crafts as well as kits containing the materials and instructions for lovely and fragrant sachets, tea cozies, scented mug coasters, and catnip mice are offered by Herbitage Farm in New Hampshire. The pleasure of these gifts is that the recipient will enjoy creating the product enclosed in the kit, while learning a new skill at the same time. Appledore Gardens in Michigan sells a kit for making your own beeswax-based hand cream (as well as beeswax nativity sets). Western Reserve in Ohio has a catalog of antique furniture kits. Arctic Trading Co. in Manitoba has kits for such unusual Indian crafts as moose-hair tufting (along with lovely examples of Indian handicrafts).

The front door is not the only place for a Christmas wreath.

Use sprigs of holly or other greens throughout your home to add a fragrant holiday touch.

For the gardeners on your list, look in the garden catalogs. Smith and Hawken in California show fine terra-cotta planters as well as garden hats, gloves, and tools that would delight any gardener. Mrs. MacGregor's Garden Shop has carved garden decorations and teakwood window boxes, while The Gardener's Collection in Ontario creates stoneware garden markers. Swinging Bridge Pottery in Virginia also makes garden markers, plus stoneware herb jars and attractive bird feeders.

There are a number of craftsmen's cooperatives that offer fine handcrafted gifts. These are professionally managed groups that offer those craftsmen who work in rural areas a chance to market their products. These artists often produce only a few pieces of any design. Berea College (Kentucky) Student Craft Industries is one of these, as is Kentucky Hills Industries. Montana Exclusive has a full-color catalog of handmade and homemade gifts ranging from coatracks in the shape of moose heads and horses to country sausage and chocolate chip cookies.

Food gifts are always welcome at Christmas, and these need not be limited to those made in your own kitchen. Unusual and hard-to-find items such as Vidalia onions and a Country Cornbread kit with cast-iron cornstick pans are shown in the catalog from Bland Farms in Georgia. Meadowbrook Herbs in Rhode Island sells their own original herb tea blends as well as utensils for making tea, and Smith and Hawken will send a dozen perfect Oregon pears.

As well as the foods themselves, cooks will appreciate kitchen accessories, which often can be found in the end pages of seed catalogs. Johnny's Selected Seeds in Maine shows a natural-fiber vegetable brush and fine kitchen knives, while Gurney Seed and Nursery in South Dakota has utensils any cook with a garden would treasure: corn cutters, vegetable slicers, and parers.

City friends without gardens can always find a place for indoor plants, and these make welcome gifts in the winter. Rhapis Gardens in Texas specializes in lady palms and other tropical exotics; Applewood Seed Company in Colorado has herb garden kits in planting sacks printed with the name of the herb. The Natural Gardening Company

Gifts of food, homemade or purchased, are always welcome.

© Obrien & Mayor/FPG International

Decorations made from dried plants are a "natural" at Christmas.

kits are designed for children. The American Girls' Series of books is full of activities from America's past, based on the stories of girls growing up in different places and periods of history. Klutz Books offer children lively and entertaining introductions to everything from juggling and blowing bubbles to cooking. These are available at bookstores and by mail from Hearthsong in California. Their catalog is filled with similar high-quality gifts for youngsters.

Although cookbooks are not an unusual gift—they are, in fact, among the most popular—you can use a cookbook as the basis for a uniquely personal gift. Combine a book on herb cookery with several packets of herbs, a wooden spoon, and a bottle of herb vinegar (see page 108). A book on growing and using fresh herbs could be grouped with simple garden tools, gloves, and a pair of garden scissors, all placed in a harvesting basket.

All-time classics of foreign cuisines can be grouped with seasonings or utensils used in that cooking style. *Come With Me to the Kasbah*, the beautifully illustrated cookbook on Moroccan cuisine, could be combined with a bag of couscous and a package of dried mint from your garden. *Cuisines of Mexico* offers a number of put-together possibilities, including your own pickled jalapeños (see page 111) or a string of dried red chili peppers (see page 107). *The Complete Book of Greek Cooking* could be combined with tahini, prepared grape leaves, or a package of pignoli nuts. A book on Chinese cooking suggests a pairing with an Oriental chopping knife or a selection of Joyce Chen's stir-fry sauces and oils.

Other how-to books are good bases for gift packages or baskets. *Natural Fragrances* would make a lovely basket combined with a potpourri jar, fragrant oils, and a bouquet or packet of dried flowers.

Think about the special interests of the people on your gift list and you will have enough ideas to last you for several Christmases. In fact, some of the best ideas often come after you have already wrapped the gift for that person, so it is wise to jot down the idea in your Christmas notebook where you'll have it ready next year.

carries terra-cotta herb planters. White Flower Farm in Connecticut ships narcissus bulbs ready for forcing into flowering plants and jasmine plants in stoneware pots ready to burst into bloom in January.

When looking for children's gifts, don't limit yourself to the standbys of toys and clothes. Craft kits and supplies and do-it-yourself toys and books will hold a child's interest long after Christmas. Several of Herbitage Farm's folk craft

A favorite doll adds a touch of childhood to the tree.

TREASURED GIFTS TO MAKE

You don't have to be an artist or skilled craftsman to create original gifts. And the nicest thing about a handmade gift is that the recipient knows you've cared enough to give them the gift of your time. The smallest handmade gift brings a personal warmth that no purchased gift can equal.

Think first of the skills and materials you have on hand. Do you sew or knit? Do you have stencil brushes and paints left from some long-ago project? Do you have woodworking tools?

If you have no tools or supplies on hand, begin with projects that do not require a major investment beyond the materials. Simple hand-sewn gifts, a small basket, old-fashioned stocking dolls, or potpourri are good starting projects that require neither expensive equipment nor special tools. Other projects require only a modest outlay, so that if you discover that you enjoy the craft, you will reuse the supplies many times. Stenciling is one of these crafts.

Other gifts can be created from nature's bounty. You don't have to live in the country to collect the dried seeds, cones, and grasses for most of the projects listed earlier in the book, any of which would make a welcome early Christmas gift. Especially for friends in the city, a balsam wreath or a box of fresh greens for decorating would be a priceless treasure. These are not fragile, they are easy to ship, and by sending them early in December you can even avoid the rush at the post office.

WOVEN RIBBON PILLOW

Little sewing is required for this elegant pillow made of satin ribbon. For variety, try mixing different types and widths of ribbon, but be sure always to use those with woven edges. Cut edges are not as durable and will not withstand the process of weaving, let alone the use of the pillow.

A 15-inch pillow form

16 yards of 1-inch-wide satin ribbon in two contrasting colors

18-inch square of velvet or other fabric in matching color

18-inch square of white muslin

Masking tape or transparent tape

Corrugated cardboard, at least 18 inches square

Straight sewing pins (common pins)

Place muslin on cardboard. Cut ribbon into 18-inch lengths and lay sixteen of one color parallel over the muslin, their edges just touching. Push a pin through each piece of ribbon into the cardboard, ½ inch from the ends of the ribbons. Press a strip of tape over the raw ends to keep them from fraying. Remove the pins and carefully stitch the ribbons to the muslin, just below the tape. Keep the ribbons straight and in line, with edges still touching. Pin to the board again through the tape, using only enough to hold the ribbons and muslin flat (you do not need a pin in each piece of ribbon this time).

Beginning close to the stitched edge, weave the remaining ribbons through the first set. Pin each cross ribbon to the cardboard at each end and be sure that each one lies close to the preceding one.

When all the ribbons have been woven, tape and stitch the remaining sides as you did the first one. Remove the tape. Place the velvet backing face down over the front of the woven square and pin them together. Stitch them together on three sides, just inside the stitching in the ribbon. This is easier if you stitch from the ribbon side, where you can always see the first stitching.

Turn the pillow right side out, squaring the corners. Pull cover over the pillow form and make sure the corners fit neatly. Turn the open edges inside and blind stitch the pillow closed.

POTPOURRI CLOTHES HANGERS

Use a purchased potpourri blend or make your own from the recipe in this book or fill these hangers with freshly dried lavendar or cedar shavings.

Wooden clothes hanger without a pants bar

2 pieces floral-print fabric, each 6 by 12 inches

1 yard matching ⅜-inch satin ribbon

2 pieces cotton or polyfiber quilt batting, each 8 by 12 inches

½ cup potpourri with extra oils and orrisroot added

Fold one fabric piece in half, with right sides facing, and stitch the long sides together to make a tube 12 inches long. Gather one end together and tie firmly with thread. Turn to the right side and repeat with the other fabric piece.

Lay the quilt batting flat and sprinkle each piece with half the potpourri. Wrap these around the wooden arms of the hangers, adjusting the tightness of the roll so they will fit inside the fabric tubes. Secure with a few wraps of thread. Pull the tubes over the batting and blind stitch together at the center. Pull the fabric toward the center so that it is shirred slightly and the ends of the fabric meet the ends of the hanger arms. Secure the ends in place with a few stitches.

Beginning at the end of the metal hook, wrap the ribbon around the metal to cover it neatly. Use the remaining ribbon to tie a bow around the base of the hook, where it meets the fabric.

CHRISTMAS POTPOURRI

Most potpourri should be kept in a container that can be covered at least half the time so that the blend can regain its strength each night and be fragrant in the daytime. This blend, however, is rich in spices and balsam sprigs, which will remain fragrant throughout the entire season even if kept in an open bowl or basket. Be sure to keep the little sprigs and needles left over from the wreaths, arrangements, and roping as well as the whole cloves that are not large enough for pomanders. Any fragrant or colorful blossom, even fallen holly and bittersweet berries, can be added to this blend.

Note: All these measurements are approximate; use more or less, or leave out ingredients that are unavailable. All plant material should be thoroughly dry.

¼ cup lemon verbena leaves

¼ cup red rose petals

½ cup balsam tips and needles

¼ cup cedar chips or tips

¼ cup dried orange peel

¼ cup coarsely broken cinnamon sticks

2 tablespoons whole cloves

2 tablespoons whole allspice

2 tablespoons rosemary leaves

2 tablespoons mint leaves

¼ cup mixed dried flowers

10 bay leaves

10 hemlock or other tiny cones

3 tablespoons orrisroot chips (not powder)

4 to 5 drops rose oil

4 to 5 drops balsam oil

2 drops cedar oil

Mix well in a large plastic bag or glass jar that will hold the potpourri, leaving plenty of air space. The jar or bag should be no more than half full. Stir or mix each day for two weeks. You can decorate the top of this blend with larger cones, sprigs of holly, or even small glass ornaments.

COVERED PICTURE FRAME

Dress up the school portrait of a child in a custom-made frame to match the bedroom of a grandmother or favorite aunt. After you have tried this project in a cotton fabric, you may dare to make one in satin, velvet, or moire taffeta.

Mat board, at least 12 by 18 inches

Matte knife or X-acto™ knife

White fabric glue (Sobo™ is preferred, since spilled drops can be wiped off with a damp cloth and it dries without staining)

Clip clothespins

Ruler

Calico fabric, at least 9 by 20 inches

Quilt batting, 6 by 8 inches

12 inches narrow satin ribbon in matching color

Cut two pieces of mat board 6 by 8 inches. Cut a rectangle from the center of one, measuring 3½ by 5 inches. To center this, measure 1¼ inches from either side, 1⅜ from the top, and 1⅝ from the bottom. Cut a 5 by 1½-inch stand from the piece cut out of the center piece.

Cut two fabric pieces, each 7 by 9 inches, then another piece 4½ by 6 inches, and another 3½ by 6 inches. Glue batting to the frame-cut mat board and let it dry before cutting out the center piece of batting.

Place frame front, batting side down, on the wrong side of one piece of fabric and center it. Mark a dot on the fabric at each of the corners of the frame opening. Remove the frame and carefully cut out the center of the fabric, leaving 1 inch inside the frame and clipping at an angle almost to the dots in each corner.

Return the mat frame front, padded side down, to the wrong side of the cut fabric. Center it carefully. Put a line of glue around the edge of the frame opening and fold the fabric to cover the edge. Be sure not to make the fabric crooked as you do this. Hold in place with clothespins. Repeat this with the outer edge, mitering the corners. Secure with clothespins. Check the right side and adjust the fabric if necessary, while the glue is wet. Take particular care with the inside corners, clipping a little farther if they do not look neat.

Cover the solid piece of mat board with the remaining large piece of fabric, using the same method. Cover the stand, using the smallest piece of fabric and folding it over to cover both sides. There will be a rough edge, but it will be glued down and on the inside where it will not show. Glue the remaining piece of fabric to cover the center of the solid mat board. The edges of the fabric do not have to meet, but be sure this piece fills the entire space, which will show when the front and back of the frame are put together.

From the remaining piece of mat board, cut three narrow strips for spacers. When the glue on the frame pieces is completely dry, remove the clothespins and glue the spacers to the top and sides at the outer edges. Glue the front of the frame over the back with the wrong sides facing. Leave the center 4 inches of the bottom without glue, and be sure to keep the glue toward the outer edges of the sides and top so the picture will slide in easily.

Spread glue on the upper third of the back side of the stand (the side with the seam)

and center it on the back of the frame. Be sure it is facing the right way and that its bottom is exactly square with the bottom of the frame, so it will stand straight.

Place the entire frame under a flat, heavy weight, such as a book, and leave overnight. When it is dry, place the ruler over the top third of the stand, and pressing down on this firmly, lift the bottom of the stand to form a neat crease. Make a bow of the ribbon and glue it near the inside corner at one side of the top on the front of the frame.

STENCILED SACHETS

Choose a stencil design that fits in a very small space for these homey little sachets. For filling, use the dried balsam needles that are left from other projects. Be sure to save the needles from this year's tree and wreaths, or you can purchase balsam needles from a supplier in Maine (see sources, page 117). You can purchase ready-cut stencils or cut your own from stencil paper. Brass stencils will last longer but are harder to use if the design has small openings.

Stencils of your choice

Stiff stencil brushes, one for each paint color

Acrylic stencil paints

Drawstring bags of unbleached muslin or 5-inch squares of unbleached muslin and narrow ribbon

Balsam needles or potpourri

A piece of cardboard small enough to fit inside the drawstring bags

If you are not using ready-made drawstring bags, fold the muslin in half and stitch around the long side and one short side. Turn bags to the right side and press flat.

Put a little acrylic paint into an old dish or piece of glass and dip the brush in it lightly. On a folded paper towel, wipe most of the paint from the brush, until it appears almost dry. Lay a stencil on a scrap of heavy paper and paint over the openings of the

stencil using an up and down circular scrubbing motion to push the bristles onto the surface of the paper. Remember to keep the brush dry; the smallest smear under the stencil means you are using too much paint. For deeper shades, go over an area several times, but don't use more paint.

When you can control the paint flow on your practice paper, you are ready to stencil on the fabric.

Slip the cardboard into the bag to protect the other side from paint and center the stencil on the bottom half of the bag. Stencil the designs, using a different brush for each color.

Clean stencils frequently with warm water. A little nail polish remover on an old toothbrush is good for removing paint buildup on brass stencils. Cleaning is important to keep paint from filling in the holes and making your design shrink as you work. Always clean on a flat surface. Be sure to clean brushes well with soap and warm water before storing them.

If you are using drawstring bags, fill them with potpourri or balsam and pull strings tight. Tie them in a double knot. If your bags do not have drawstrings, fill them a little over half full and tie with ribbons, using a bow knot.

These sachets can be piled in a basket and given to holiday guests as they leave. Or, a small basket of them makes a very nice gift.

© Hanson Carroll

GIFTS FROM A COUNTRY KITCHEN

No gift is as welcome, especially at the holidays, as one you've created in your own kitchen. If you have made your own harvest—or that of a farmers' market—into preserves during the fall, you already have a good beginning. But even closer to Christmas, pumpkins, oranges, lemons, limes, cranberries, and other products are at their peak so don't forget to include them when you are making preserves.

By combining preserves, vinegars, and herb blends, which you can make ahead, with a loaf of tea bread and a few decorative cookies as a finishing touch, you can give elegant food baskets without overcrowding your holiday season. These personal gifts will be enjoyed and appreciated all through the winter.

© William Seitz

LEMON NUTMEG COOKIES

1 cup sifted flour

½ cup cornstarch

¼ teaspoon salt

½ teaspoon freshly ground nutmeg

½ cup plus 2 tablespoons unsalted butter, softened

½ cup confectioner's sugar

1 tablespoon freshly grated lemon rind

Sift together flour, cornstarch, salt, and nutmeg. Cream butter with sugar and lemon until fluffy. Add dry ingredients and beat until smooth. Roll teaspoonfuls of dough into balls and place on ungreased cookie sheets. Flatten with the bottom of a glass that has been dipped in confectioners' sugar. Bake at 325°F for 15 minutes, or until cookies are golden at the edges. Cool a minute or two before removing from cookie sheets and continue cooling on racks.

Makes approximately 3 dozen small cookies.

BRANDIED FRUIT

Fresh or canned peach halves

Fresh or canned pear halves

Canned pineapple rings

Thinly sliced lemon

Peach or apricot brandy

Layer fruit carefully in a French-style canning jar with a hinged lid. Pour peach or apricot brandy over the fruit to fill the jar and seal. Let stand one week before using. Whole dark cherries or apricot halves may be added or used to replace other fruits.

MINCEMEAT BARS

½ cup margarine

½ cup sugar

1 egg

⅓ cup molasses

2 cups flour

½ teaspoon baking soda

½ teaspoon baking powder

¼ teaspoon cinnamon

¼ teaspoon allspice

¼ teaspoon salt

1 cup well-drained mincemeat

Cream margarine with sugar. Add egg and molasses and beat until light. Sift together flour, baking soda, baking powder, cinnamon, allspice, and salt and add alternately with mincemeat, stirring until well blended. Pour into a well-greased 13-inch × 9-inch pan and bake at 350°F for 30 minutes or until center is firm and springs back when touched. Cool and cut into squares. Seal in a tightly covered container to store.

Makes about 32 bars.

PUMPKIN COOKIES

1 cup shortening

1½ cups sugar

1 egg

1 cup mashed cooked pumpkin

1 teaspoon baking soda

3½ cups sifted flour

½ teaspoon salt

½ teaspoon cinnamon

½ teaspoon nutmeg

½ teaspoon ginger

1 cup raisins

Cream shortening with sugar and add egg. Mix well and add pumpkin. Stir to blend. Sift together baking soda, flour, salt, cinnamon, nutmeg, ginger, and raisins and add to blended mixture. Drop by teaspoonfuls on greased cookie sheets. Bake at 400°F for 8 to 10 minutes. These cookies stay moist and keep very well.

Makes approximately 6 dozen cookies.

SUGAR COOKIES

½ *cup butter*

¾ *cup sugar*

1 egg

½ *teaspoon vanilla*

1 tablespoon milk

1¼ *cups flour*

¼ *teaspoon salt*

¼ *teaspoon baking powder*

Cream butter and sugar until light. Add egg and vanilla, beat again, and add milk. Sift together flour, salt, and baking powder and stir into butter mixture to make a smooth dough. Chill well and roll out on floured board. Cut in shapes and bake cookies until lightly browned. Cool on racks.

Decorate with red- and green-colored sugars or with decorator's frosting, which can be purchased in tubes complete with cake decorating tips. Small, colored candies, such as cinnamon hots and gum drops may be pressed into the center of the cookies before baking. Brushing the dough with egg white will make the surface of the cookie glossy.

Size may vary, but yields 2 cookie sheets.

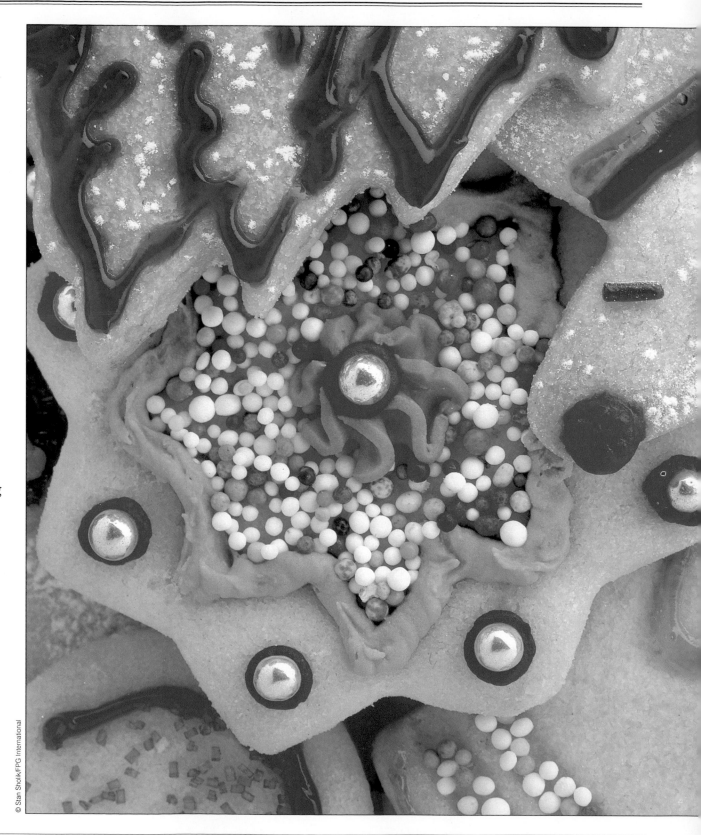

© Stan Sholik/FPG International

MOLDED GERMAN CHRISTMAS COOKIES

3 cups flour

½ teaspoon cloves

1 ½ teaspoons cinnamon

1 teaspoon ginger

½ teaspoon nutmeg

½ teaspoon allspice

Pinch of baking powder

Pinch of salt

1 ¼ cups margarine or butter

3 tablespoons milk

¼ cup ground almonds

1 cup firmly packed brown sugar

Combine flour, cloves, cinnamon, ginger, nutmeg, allspice, baking powder, and salt and cut in butter until the mixture is fine and crumbly. Add milk, almonds, and sugar.

Dust the carved side of wooden cookie molds with flour. Grease the cookie sheet lightly. Roll dough ½ inch thick and cut into rectangles the size of the molds. Lay a piece of dough over the carved side of a mold and roll firmly with rolling pin until the dough is pressed into the carved design. Remove dough carefully and place, design side up, on cookie sheets. Trim edges if necessary. Dust mold again with flour before reusing. Bake 25 minutes in a 350°F oven. Remove from sheets and cool on racks.

Makes approximately 2 dozen cookies.

APPLE-CRANBERRY BREAD

½ cup margarine

1¼ cups sugar

2 eggs, beaten

1 tablespoon buttermilk

2 cups flour

1 teaspoon baking powder

1 teaspoon baking soda

1 teaspoon salt

1 cup finely chopped, peeled apple

1 cup coarsely chopped cranberries, drained

1 tablespoon grated lemon peel

½ cup chopped pecans

1 teaspoon vanilla

½ teaspoon cinnamon

½ teaspoon allspice

Cream margarine and sugar, then beat in eggs and buttermilk. Sift together flour, baking powder, baking soda, and salt and add alternately with fruit. Add remaining ingredients. Pour into greased loaf pan and bake 50 to 60 minutes at 350°F.

Makes 1 large or 2 small loaves.

DATE NUT TEA BREAD

1 pound chopped dates

1½ cups boiling water

2 teaspoons baking soda

2¼ cups flour

½ teaspoon baking powder

1½ cups sugar

½ teaspoon salt

1 egg

1 tablespoon vegetable oil

1 teaspoon vanilla

1 cup chopped walnuts

Combine dates, water, and baking soda. In another bowl combine flour, baking powder, sugar, and salt. In a third bowl, beat egg and add oil and vanilla. Add egg and date mixture alternately to dry ingredients, stir in walnuts, and pour into two small loaf pans lined with waxed paper. Bake 1¼ hours or until springy and firm. Remove from pans immediately after taking the loaves from the oven and peel off waxed paper while still hot. When cool, wrap in waxed paper and then in foil. This sturdy bread ships well and can be kept for several weeks.

Makes 1 large or 2 small loaves.

CHARLESTON BENNE WAFERS

¾ *cup raw sesame seeds*

¾ *cup unsalted butter*

1 cup brown sugar, packed

1 egg

1 cup flour

½ *teaspoon baking powder*

1 teaspoon vanilla

In a dry frying pan, lightly toast seeds over low heat. Pour them from the pan the minute they begin to toast and allow to cool.

Cream butter and sugar until soft, add egg, and beat until fluffy. Combine flour and baking powder and add with vanilla and sesame seeds. Mix well.

Drop by spoonfuls onto greased cookie sheets about an inch apart. Bake 12 to 15 minutes at 325°F until they are lightly browned. Leave on the sheets for a minute after removing them from the oven, then remove them to racks to cool. These may be stored in tightly sealed tins.

Makes approximately 3 to 4 dozen wafers.

PRALINES

3 cups sugar

1 cup light cream

Dash of salt

1 cup light brown sugar

3 cups pecan pieces

Combine sugar, cream, and salt in a heavy saucepan and cook to 234°F. Meanwhile, melt brown sugar in a saucepan over very low heat. Add to the syrup with the pecans. Bring to a rolling boil and cook for two minutes, stirring constantly. Drop by teaspoonfuls onto waxed paper squares and allow to cool. When they are firm and cold, wrap each in its paper square and store.

Makes about 1½ dozen pralines.

TAFFY KISSES

1 cup sugar

2 tablespoons cornstarch

¾ *cup light corn syrup*

½ *cup water*

2 tablespoons margarine

½ *teaspoon salt*

1 teaspoon flavoring (orange, lemon, mint, or other)

Mix sugar and cornstarch in a large, heavy saucepan. Stir in remaining ingredients, except for flavoring. Cook over medium heat, stirring constantly, until sugar is completely dissolved. Continue cooking without stirring until temperature reaches 260°F. Remove from heat, and after all boiling has stopped, stir in flavoring. Pour onto lightly greased cookie sheets and let stand until it is cool enough to handle. Grease hands and pull taffy, stretching it, doubling it over, and stretching it again until it is glossy and pale colored. Form into ropes about ½ inch in diameter and cut with scissors into 1-inch pieces. Wrap individually in waxed paper, twisting ends like firecrackers.

Makes about 1 pound.

LEMON OATMEAL BARS

⅓ *cup margarine*

⅔ *cup brown sugar, packed*

1 egg

1 cup sifted flour

¼ *teaspoon baking soda*

1¼ *cups rolled oats*

½ *cup milk*

6 ounces butterscotch chips

Blend margarine and brown sugar together; add egg and mix well. Sift together flour and baking soda and add to butter with oats and milk. Stir in butterscotch chips and pour into a greased 10-inch × 5-inch × 3-inch pan which has been lined with waxed paper. Bake at 375°F for 35 to 40 minutes. Meanwhile, make lemon syrup (see recipe below). Pour hot syrup over immediately after removing from the oven. Cool thoroughly and cut into bars.

To make lemon syrup:

¼ *cup sugar*

1 tablespoon lemon juice

1 tablespoon grated fresh lemon peel

Bring sugar and juice to a boil, stirring constantly. When sugar has dissolved, remove from heat immediately and add peel.

Makes 2 dozen 2-inch × 1-inch bars.

© Nancy S. Dituri/Envision

DRIED PEPPER STRINGS

Fresh red hot peppers

Jute cord

A heavy needle

Thread the cord into a needle and make a large loop in the free end. String the peppers onto the cord. Tie the cord around the final pepper and knot firmly. Hang the peppers in a dry, airy place until crisp.

FOUR-FRUIT MARMALADE

1 orange

1 lemon

1 medium-size grapefruit

½ cup water

⅛ teaspoon baking soda

5 cups sugar

½ bottle liquid fruit pectin

¼ cup sliced maraschino cherries

Peel the fruit and remove half of the white rinds found inside the peels. Sliver the remaining peel and combine with water and baking soda. Bring to a boil and simmer, covered, for twenty minutes. Meanwhile, chop the fruit, removing the seeds. Add the fruit to the rinds, cover, and simmer ten minutes longer. Measure 3 cups of this fruit into a large saucepan.

Add the sugar to the fruit and mix well. Over high heat, bring to a full rolling boil. Boil for one minute, stirring constantly. Remove from the heat and stir in the pectin all at once. Stir for five minutes, skimming off the foam. Add the cherries and spoon into sterilized jars, taking care to get even amounts of fruit in each. Seal the jars and process for five minutes in boiling water to cover.

Makes seven half-pint jars.

PENNSYLVANIA DUTCH CHOW CHOW

2 cups very small green
   tomatoes, quartered

2 cups very small cucumbers
   (4-inch maximum), cut
   in ½-inch slices

2 cups tiny pickling onions,
   peeled

2 cups firm, fresh cauliflower,
   broken into florets

2 firm green peppers, cut in
   1-inch squares

2 firm, sweet red peppers, cut
   in 1-inch squares

2 cups fresh-picked green
   beans, cut in 1-inch
   lengths

1 cup pickling salt

¾ cup white flour

¼ cup ground mustard

1½ teaspoons turmeric

1½ cups sugar

6 cups cider vinegar

Mix the vegetables in a large glass bowl or stainless-steel pot and sprinkle with the salt. Cover with very cold water and let stand overnight. Drain, cover with cold water, and bring just to the boiling point. Drain well.

Combine the remaining ingredients with a wire whisk to make a smooth sauce; cook over moderate heat, stirring constantly until thick and smooth. Add the vegetables and slowly bring just to the boiling point. The vegetables should not become soft. Stir often to prevent the sauce from scorching the bottom of the pan. Spoon into hot, sterilized jars and seal immediately. Process for ten minutes in boiling water.

Makes ten half-pint jars.

PEACH HONEY

3 pounds ripe peaches

sugar

Peel the peaches and cut in half, removing the pits. Mash thoroughly and measure. Add 2 cups sugar for each cup of fruit. Bring to a boil over very low heat and simmer until thick and clear, stirring constantly. This takes about an hour, and it scorches easily, so be sure to keep stirring.

Pour into hot, sterilized jars and seal immediately. Process in boiling water for ten minutes to seal.

HERB VINEGARS

Sprigs of fresh herbs

Vinegars: white distilled,
   wine, and cider (see
   instructions below)

Tall, thin jars

Fill jar about one-third full of herbs, then fill with vinegar. Seal and store in a shady place for two weeks before using. Use the following combinations of herbs and vinegars:

Mint and cider vinegar

Basil and red wine vinegar

Marjoram and red wine
   vinegar

Oregano and red wine vinegar

Purple basil and white
   distilled vinegar

Tarragon and white wine
   vinegar

Salad burnet and red wine
   vinegar

Lemon balm and white
   distilled vinegar

Chive blossoms and white
   distilled vinegar

PICKLED CARROT STICKS

1 pound peeled carrots

¾ cup white distilled vinegar

¾ cup water

½ cup sugar

2 teaspoons mixed pickling spices

Cut carrots into pencil-thick sticks. Cook five minutes in boiling water and drain. Meanwhile, combine the remaining ingredients and simmer for five minutes. Stand the carrots in hot, sterilized jars and pour in the vinegar mix up to ½ inch from the top. Seal and process the jars in boiling water to cover for five minutes.

Makes four half-pint jars.

PUMPKIN PICKLES

2½ cups sugar

2½ cups white distilled vinegar

3 cups water

4 cinnamon sticks

1 tablespoon whole cloves

4 pounds pumpkin

Combine sugar, water, vinegar, and spices and boil for ten minutes to make a syrup. Peel the pumpkin and cut into 1-inch squares. You will have about 6 cups. Boil in the syrup for five minutes, then cover and let stand for one hour. Simmer slowly about one hour until the pumpkin is transparent. Remove the spices. Spoon the pickles into hot, sterilized jars and cover with the syrup. Seal and process in boiling water to cover for fifteen minutes.

Makes six half-pint jars.

PICKLED JALAPEÑOS

Fresh jalapeño peppers

Cider vinegar

Wash the peppers and prick each in two places with the tip of a paring knife. Pack in hot, sterilized jars as snugly as possible. Meanwhile, heat the vinegar just to the boiling point. Fill the jars with hot vinegar and seal. Process ten minutes in boiling water to cover.

SPICED GRAPE JELLY

3½ cups grape juice

½ cup cider vinegar

1 cinnamon stick

10 whole cloves

7 cups sugar

½ bottle liquid fruit pectin

Combine the grape juice, vinegar, and spices in a saucepan and bring just to the simmering point. Turn off the heat and allow to stand, covered, for ten minutes. Remove the spices.

Add sugar to the juice and mix well. Place over high heat and bring to a boil, stirring constantly. Stir in the pectin all at once, bring to a full, rolling boil, and boil hard for one minute, stirring constantly. Remove from the heat, skim off the foam, and pour into sterilized jars. Seal immediately.

Makes nine half-pint jars.

CALICO HEART (CUT 2)

WALNUT SHELL LAMB

1. Cut the needed amount of felt from pattern provided.
2. Placement of felt on walnut shell half.
3. Completed Walnut Shell Lamb.

HEAD (CUT 1)

FEET (CUT 4)

TAIL (CUT 1)

PAPER CUTOUTS

YARN DOLL

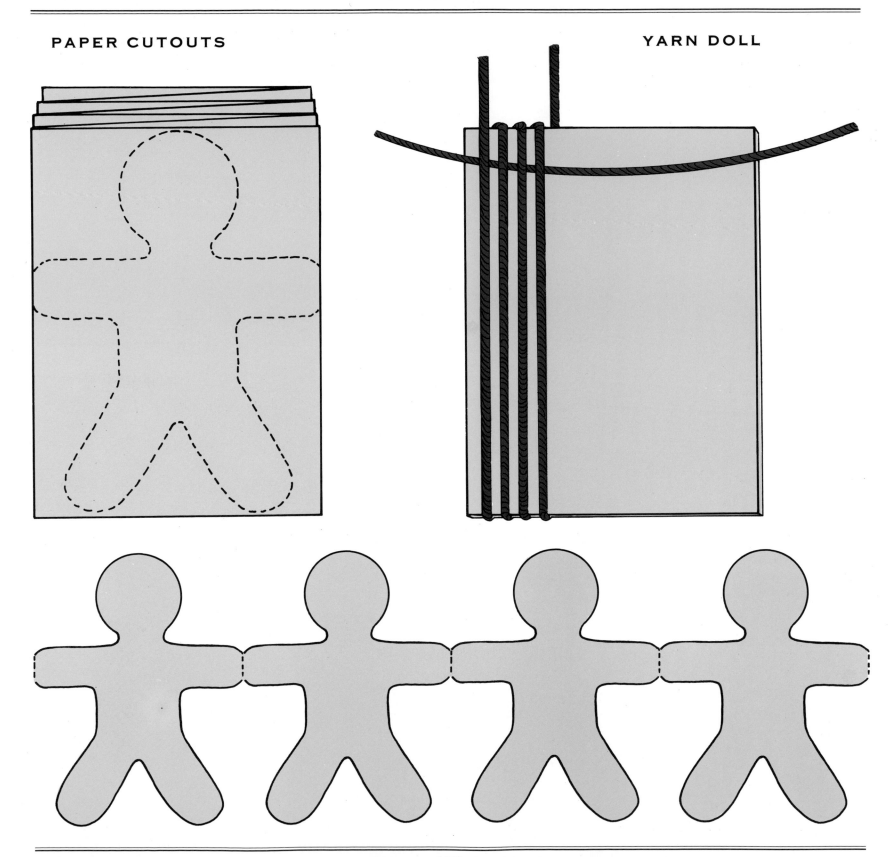

A BASKET OF VELVET FRUITS

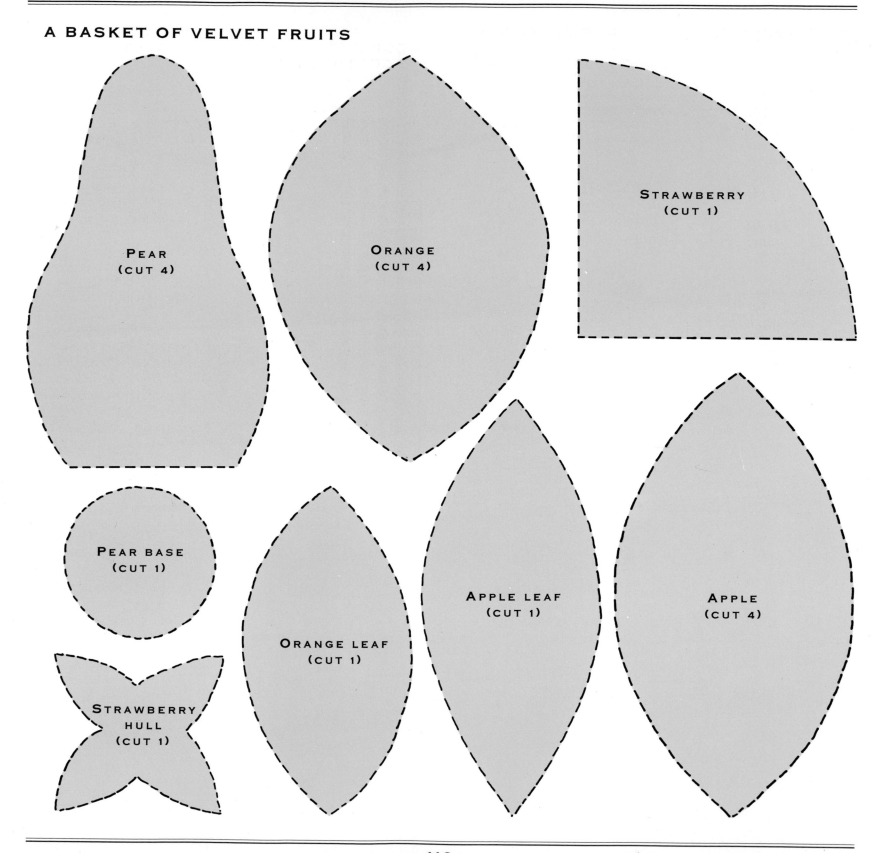

PEAR
(CUT 4)

ORANGE
(CUT 4)

STRAWBERRY
(CUT 1)

PEAR BASE
(CUT 1)

APPLE LEAF
(CUT 1)

APPLE
(CUT 4)

ORANGE LEAF
(CUT 1)

STRAWBERRY
HULL
(CUT 1)

SOURCES

Herbitage Farm
Old Homestead Highway
Richmond, NH 03470
Potpourri oils, dried flowers,
craft instructions
(catalog $1.00)

Maine Balsam Fir Products
P.O. Box 123
West Paris, ME 04289
Fragrant balsam needles,
small cones

Rosemary House
120 South Market Street
Mechanicsburg, PA 17055
Potpourri supplies
(catalog $1.00)

MUSEUM SHOPS

American Indian Archaeological Institute
P.O. Box 260
Curtis Road
Washington, CT 06793
American Indian crafts

The Fort at #4
Route 11, Box 336
Charlestown, NH 03603
Colonial items and black-
smithing

Old Sturbridge Village
One Old Sturbridge Village
   Road
Sturbridge, MA 01566
Early American crafts and
gifts

The Western Reserve
Box 206A
Bath, Ohio 44210
Reproduction furniture kits
(catalog $2.00)

CRAFT COOPERATIVES AND COLLECTIONS

Arctic Trading Company
Kelsey and Bernier Streets
Churchill, Manitoba
Canada R0B 0E0
Northwest Indian crafts and
kits

Berea College Student Craft
   Industries
CPO 2347
Berea, KY 40404
Folk arts and mountain crafts

Kentucky Hills Industries
Pine Knot, KY 42635
Woodwork and mountain
crafts
(catalog $2.00)

Montana Exclusive
29 Border Lane #1
Bozeman, MT 59715
Pottery, wood, foods, and toys

FOOD AND KITCHEN ACCESSORIES

Bland Farms
P.O. Box 506
Glennville, GA 30427-0506
Cornbread kit, condiments,
and onions

Johnny's Selected Seeds
Foss Hill Road
Albion, ME 04910
Unusual kitchen utensils and
knives

Gurney Seed and Nursery Co.
Yankton, SD 57079
Kitchen utensils

Joyce Chen Products
411 Waverly Oaks Road
Waltham, MA 02154
Non-stick woks, Chinese
sauces, and cooking utensils

Meadowbrook Herb Garden
Route 138
Wyoming, RI 02898
Herb teas and blends
(catalog $1.00)

HERB FARMS

Appledore Gardens
Box 36125
Grosse Pointe Farms, MI 48236
Beeswax kits and gifts

Betsy Williams
155 Chestnut Street
Andover, MA 01810
Herb and dried flower wreaths

Hartman's Herb Farm
Old Dana Road
Barre, MA 01005
Calendars and herbal gifts
(catalog $2.00)

Herbitage Farm
Old Homestead Highway
Richmond, NH 03470
Herb and folk craft kits
(catalog $1.00)

Rosemary House
120 South Market Street
Mechanicsburg, PA 17055
Herb blends and crafts
(catalog $1.00)

GIFTS FOR CHILDREN

Hearth Song
P.O. Box B
Sebastopol, CA 95473-0601
Creative and unusual children's gifts

Pleasant Company
8400 Fairway Place
Middleton, WI 53562
"American Girls" books and activity portfolios

FOR INDOOR GARDENERS

Shepherd's Garden Seeds
30 Irene Street
Torrington, CT 06790-6657
Peppermills and gourmet peppercorns

Applewood Seed Company
5380 Vivian Street
Arvada, CO 80002
Indoor herb garden kits

The Natural Gardening Company
217 San Anselmo Ave.
San Anselmo, CA 94960
Terra-cotta planters

White Flower Farm
Litchfield, CT 06759-0050
Narcissus bulbs and forcing bowls

Rhapis Gardens
P.O. Box 287
Gregory, TX 78359
Lady palms, exotic plants, and pots

GIFT BOOKS

The Complete Book of Greek Cooking
St. Paul's Greek Orthodox Cathedral
Hempstead, NY 11511
(Published by Harper & Row)

Come With Me to the Kasbah: A Cook's Tour of Morocco
by Kitty Morse
La Caravane
P.O. Box 433
Vista, CA 92083
($24.95 plus $3.00 shipping)

The Cuisines of Mexico
by Diana Kennedy
(Published by Harper and Row)

Natural Fragrances
by Gail Duff
(Published by Garden Way/Storey)

GARDEN SUPPLIERS

The Gardener's Collection
Deline Lake, P.O. Box 243
Sydenham, Ontario
Canada K0H 2T0
Stoneware garden markers

Mrs. MacGregor's Garden Shop
4801 First Street North
Arlington, VA 22203
Teak window boxes and accessories

Smith and Hawken
25 Corte Madera
Mill Valley, CA 94941
Garden accessories and gifts

Swinging Bridge Pottery
S.R. 2, Box 395
Criglersville, VA 22727
Bird feeders and garden markers